# MAN IN AN
# ARTIFICIAL LANDSCAPE

## THE MARVELS OF CIVILIZATION
## IN IMPERIAL ROMAN LITERATURE

# MNEMOSYNE

## BIBLIOTHECA CLASSICA BATAVA

COLLEGERUNT

W. DEN BOER • W. J. VERDENIUS • R. E. H. WESTENDORP BOERMA
BIBLIOTHECAE FASCICULOS EDENDOS CURAVIT
W. J. VERDENIUS, HOMERUSLAAN 53, ZEIST

SUPPLEMENTUM VICESIMUM QUINTUM

ZOJA PAVLOVSKIS

## MAN IN AN
## ARTIFICIAL LANDSCAPE
### THE MARVELS OF CIVILIZATION
### IN IMPERIAL ROMAN LITERATURE

LUGDUNI BATAVORUM E. J. BRILL MCMLXXIII

# MAN IN AN ARTIFICIAL LANDSCAPE

## THE MARVELS OF CIVILIZATION IN IMPERIAL ROMAN LITERATURE

BY

ZOJA PAVLOVSKIS

LUGDUNI BATAVORUM E. J. BRILL MCMLXXIII

Work on this monograph has been facilitated by two grants, received from The Research Foundation of the State University of New York, and held in the summers of 1970 and 1971.

ISBN    90 04 03643 1

PRINTED IN THE NETHERLANDS

*Harry Caplan munusculum*

# MAN IN AN ARTIFICIAL LANDSCAPE

No reader of ancient literature will regard Statius or the younger Pliny as one of the greatest Latin authors. On the other hand, the usual modern tendency to dismiss most of the writers of the Silver Age as derivative and contrived[1] does little justice to the originality of many of them, and particularly Statius, who may well have been the first to devote whole poems to the praise of technological progress, as well as the delights of a life spent in a setting not natural but improved by man's skill. Pliny, in his turn, successfully introduced this poetic topic to prose.

How difficult it is to do justice to such a literary theme can be seen in our own time. Convincing poetry, as well as other works of art, dealing with technological progress are scarce, although attempts in this direction obviously should be relevant and ought to fill a need.[2] The attitude of modern artists toward technology is, however, ambivalent at best — at worst, fearful and pessimistic.[3] Even an artist

---

[1] Such opinions are widespread, and Statius particularly has suffered from them, especially in the past. See, for instance, J. W. Duff, *A Literary History of Rome in the Silver Age* (2nd ed., London 1960), 393 and elsewhere on Statius. Rather atypical is the favorable opinion of Alfred Biese, *Die Entwicklung des Naturgefühls bei den Griechen und Römern*, pt. 2 (Kiel 1884), 156-7:

> Statius versteht mit kräftigen Strichen zu schildern; seine Liebe zum bescheidenen Landleben, die Bewunderung der freien wie auch der durch die Kunst gemeisterten Natur, ein fein beobachtendes Auge für Spiegelung oder im Laube spielende Lichter oder die Schatten, welche auf Meer und Feld dem darüber hinziehenden Kranichschwarm nachhuschen: alles das zeugt von einer gesteigerten Innerlichkeit des Empfindens. Seine Skizzen gewähren uns einen Einblick in die Gefühlsweise der damaligen gebildeten Welt und entrollen uns durch die Villenbeschreibungen ein interessantes Kulturbild.

Commendable is the recent work of Hubert Cancik, *Untersuchungen zur lyrischen Kunst des P. Papinius Statius* (Hildesheim 1965), which does much to reveal the originality and genuineness of the poetic inspiration of Statius' *Silvae*. Cancik, 40-3, sees Statius as a mannerist, and defines mannerism as a predilection for irreality and illusion.

[2] The Futurists made some abortive attempts in this direction. Other modern artists have, for the most part, been either ambivalent in their attitude toward technological progress (for instance, Stephen Spender in "The Landscape Near an Aerodrome") or completely hostile to it (for instance, Hans Magnus Enzensberger in "an alle fernsprechteilnehmer" and Jean Dubuffet in his painting "The Automobile, Flower of Industry," in the possession of Richard L. Feigen & Co., New York). These examples are chosen at random from the very great number available.

[3] Modern distrust of the idea of progress is well illustrated by works such as Spengler's *Der Mensch und die Technik* and Freud's *Das Unbehagen in der Kultur*.

who has not lost faith in progress, once he sets himself the task of extolling some technological marvel, runs into considerable practical problems: frequently he is ignorant of the intricacies of engineering and other highly specialized technical matters, and easily risks being dull to his equally uninitiated public; or else his work will be interesting for a short time only, since machines and inventions are fast supplanted by still other machines and inventions, and thus abandoned and forgotten.[4]

Statius avoids all these dangers. His occasional poems, the *Silvae*, are quite readable even now, and perhaps more so than his undertakings in the grand epic genre. The secret of his success may lie not only in the relatively static character of ancient technology, but in the feeling of great optimism that pervades most of the *Silvae*. Statius feels and expresses a genuine joy in man's subjugation of nature.

Ever since Hesiod poets had spoken of a Golden Age, a time irretrievably lost in the dim past. In the *Silvae* a happiness similar to that of the Golden Age appears to have briefly returned in an unusual guise—that of life in the midst of contemporary Roman civilization, with its superior baths, roads, and gardens.[5] Man the creator of comfort adapts nature for his purposes. Refinement is no longer regarded as sinful.[6] The desire of Statius' patrons to have the poet praise their technologically impressive possessions testifies to the

---

[4] Especially if the work in question has overtones of a particular political ideology, as is frequently the case. See, for instance, Gabriele D'Annunzio's "A una torpediniera nell' Adriatico."

[5] As early as the principate of Nero do poets declare that the Golden Age, such as the Fourth Eclogue of Virgil predicted, has, in fact, arrived. See Calpurnius Siculus 1. 33-88 and the Einsiedeln Eclogue 2. 23-38.—On the expression of the idea of the Golden Age in Roman pastoral, as well as Roman elegy and epigram, see Jean Hubaux, *Les thèmes bucoliques dans la poésie latine* (Académie Royale de Belgique, Classe des Lettres, Mémoires XXIX, fasc. 1, Bruxelles 1930), especially 134-55, "Les thèmes Romains dans la poésie bucolique." Pp. 196-213, Hubaux discusses Calpurnius as a propagator of this idea.

[6] The feeling that man's pursuit of activities for which he is not equipped by nature is sinful is so commonplace that it hardly needs extensive documentation. An obvious example is a passage such as Horace *Carm.* 1. 3. 25-40. On the other hand, the concomitant of an acceptance of the ideal of the Golden Age is the acceptance of a rather high standard of material comfort. The Golden Age cannot be really primitive. See A. O. Lovejoy and George Boas, *History of Primitivism and Related Ideas*, I, *Primitivism and Related Ideas in Antiquity* (Baltimore 1935), *passim*, who distinguish between "hard" and "soft" primitivism—the former a truly primitive state, harsh and difficult, the latter, an idealized existence close to nature, simple but free from care and toil.

optimistic sentiment of the day.[7] Statius' own views, we may suspect, were in accord with those of his patrons. Hence the convincing tone which the *Silvae* succeed in communicating. Technology delights — and why should it not? It is the product of a modern, superior way of life.

> Prisca iuvent alios, ego me nunc denique natum
> gratulor: haec aetas moribus apta meis (*A. A.* 3. 121-2),

said Ovid,[8] possibly tongue in cheek.[9] Yet his words are not merely roguish. They reflect the pride of the Roman citizen in the modern conditions of the well-ordered Empire.[10]

The novelty of Statius' attitude will become apparent when we look at the work of some of his predecessors. Many of them also approve of material comfort, but at the same time emphasize the simplicity necessary for happiness. The uncomplicated satisfaction of one's needs is described very effectively by authors such as Lucretius,[11] who, however, does not choose to place his Epicurean company in the midst of inclement weather, which would make the amenities of civilization welcome and even necessary.[12] Horace, another poet fond of comfort, follows Alcaeus in picturing how cozily one can be sheltered from winter storm[13] or summer heat.[14] Good firewood helps Horace to pass the winter, as does the *quadrimum merum*, yet all these pleasures are time-honored and relatively simple. They have not changed since the

---

[7] Karl Schefold, *Pompeianische Malerei, Sinn und Ideengeschichte* (Basel 1952), seeks to show a connection between Roman faith in technical progress and in happiness. (This, incidentally, is not the principal thesis of the book.) See especially 17-8, where Schefold refers to Ernst Buschor, *Technisches Sehen* (Munich 1952), and his concept of "das technische Sehen," that is, man's urge to shape nature and improve on her.

[8] I have been unable to read the article of G. Krókowski, "De poeta elegiaco urbis amatore," *Eos* XLIII 1 (1948-9), 167-85, in which, according to *L'Année Philologique* XIX (1948), 109, the author demonstrates how Propertius and Ovid create for what they have to say an artificial background based on the plastic arts, as well as myths.

[9] Cf. Horace *Serm.* 2. 7. 22-7 and *Epod.* 2, where the speakers pay lip-service to ancient simplicity, continuing, however, to derive great satisfaction from their participation in modern life.

[10] Already in the earlier periods of Roman civilization do we encounter an insistence on triumphing over the irregularities of nature. To mention only two instances of this tendency, Roman roads were laid out as straight as possible, and the set-up of the Roman military camp was unchangeably regular.

[11] See passages such as *De Rerum Natura* 2. 20-33.

[12] In a different mood, 5. 330-7, 1448-57, Lucretius approves of the progress of inventions.

[13] *Carm.* 1. 9, cf. Alcaeus Z 14 (the numbering of Alcaeus is that used by Denys Page, *Sappho and Alcaeus*, Oxford 1955). Page follows the tradition of discerning a resemblance between this poem of Alcaeus and Horace 1. 9.

[14] *Carm.* 1. 17.

3

time of Alcaeus. Technology may as well not have progressed during the past several thousand years, so slight is its influence on the pictures of happy life as Horace or Lucretius see it. Statius' predecessors place happiness in primitive or almost primitive conditions. Nature grants man necessities but not luxuries, and any possibility of a recurrence of the Golden Age is attended by freedom from hard work and danger,[15] but also by a kind of rustic austerity.[16]

[15] As in Virgil *Ecl.* 4 and Horace *Epod.* 16.

[16] Yet in Virgil's poetry there are at least two passages in which we can see signs of the later fascination with the blessings of a luxurious civilization. The first of these passages is notorious: the purple and yellow sheep of *Ecl.* 4 often offend the taste of the reader prepared to be elevated by the Messianic Eclogue (no matter what his opinion on the identity of the Child, the reader expects this poem to be uniformly lofty and grave). These vividly colored animals fulfill an important purpose in the poem: they indicate that in the anticipated Golden Age nature will be capable of much more than now, so that luxury will be not a sin but a readily available delight. (The strange comment of Macrobius, *Sat.* 3. 7. 2, and of Servius Danielis on *Ecl.* 4. 43, "Hoc in honorem vel laudem Augusti refert, traditur enim in libris Etruscorum, si hoc animal miro et insolito colore fuerit inductum, portendi imperatori rerum omnium felicitatem,"—*sic* Macrobius, Servius' wording differs slightly from the above—no matter whether founded on actual knowledge of the prophetic books or not, need not disturb us here. In the context of the poem, the passage on the sheep appears not as a supernatural portent but as a culmination of a whole series of glorious gifts which eventually will become available to man. *Assyrium vulgo nascetur amomum*, we are told earlier, in line 15.)

The second passage is *G.* 2. 155-64. It too comes as the culmination of an extensive passage, that dealing with the characteristics which make Italy the most wonderful country in the world. Not only is Italy less dangerous than the lands of the fabulous East—it is also less wild, better cultivated, and can boast of such marvels of human skill as great walled cities and channels connecting great bodies of water. Although the *Georgics* advocate a return to rustic simplicity, in this passage, at least, Virgil cares not to observe the literary convention which condemned man's architectural accomplishments as unnatural and sinful. (Cf. Horace *Carm.* 2. 15. 1-11, and 3. 1. 33-4.) The reason for Virgil's acceptance of channels and fortifications may be that, in the *Georgics* at least,

> ... la notion abstraite élaborée [par les stoïciens] dans les écoles des villes passe dans un registre inaccoutumé. L'ordre, c'est de revêtir de bois une montagne, c'est d'irriguer une terre sèche ... Et certes l'idée d'un monde investi par le divin est commune chez les Anciens, mais ce divin on s'unit à lui dans la contemplation: ce n'est jamais par les mains qu'il monte des choses dans l'homme. (Jacques Perret, *Virgile*, Éditions du Seuil 1959, pp. 70, 73.)

Elsewhere too in the poetry of Virgil's time we meet admiration of technological progress. For instance, a Greek, Antipater of Thessalonica (*Anth. Graeca* 9. 418), praises the recent invention of the watermill. But the poetic treatments of such topics are scattered and brief before Statius, although, no doubt, technology has delighted man ever since there has been man—and technology. The ancient world found its tasks sweetened by various inventions, ranging from the practical to the fanciful (in addition to standard works such as *A History of Technology*, II, various authors, Oxford 1956, see the entertaining book of R. S. Brumbaugh, *Ancient Greek Gadgets and Machines*,

In Statius' own time, Martial likes to speak, in a Horatian vein, of the blessings of a well-fed life on the farm.[17] As other satirists,[18] Martial too will give up a complex city life for a simpler and more restful existence in the country. Yet along with the deprecation of the luxurious, unnatural, life, the theme of coziness continues going through Roman literature as a parallel strain. Life is to be simple, but not too simple: one cannot enjoy the wretchedness of truly primitive living conditions. One wants not too much, but a modicum sufficient for a modest standard of comfort. Along with Lucretius and Horace, Martial does not believe in ascetic self-denial. Roman authors advise giving up ambition and luxury, but only for the equally great satisfactions of a quiet coziness. They are sceptical about the happiness of a really primitive state[19] and recommend not it but rustic simplicity such as prevails in the small Italian hamlets and townships.

Yet once we make the assumption that without some degree of civilization man cannot be happy, the road lies open for the acceptance of civilization as, on the whole, a splendid thing. The same love of contentment and coziness which the critics of the complicated urban life profess, provides the ground on which rests Statius' glorification of technical achievement, for such achievement serves comfort and coziness. As we shall see, the theme of escape from the city frequently appears in the *Silvae*, but unlike Horace, who used to retire to a simple Sabine farm, Statius' patrons take vacations at elaborate villas, close to nature's beauties yet immune to her harshness. What is more, their country estates have been developed in such ways that their dwellers do not rightly know where nature ends and art begins, and consequently can enjoy the illusion of holding nature in a kind of magical grasp, completely at their command.[20]

New York 1966), and the idea of progress is hardly a recent invention (see Lovejoy and Boas, ch. VII, "Anti-Primitivism in Greek Literature: Eighth to First Centuries B. C.," and ch. XII, "Anti-Primitivism and the Idea of Progress in Later Classical Literature").

[17] As in *Epigr.* 3. 58 and elsewhere. (The numbering of Martial's poems adopted here is that of Ludwig Friedlaender, *M. Valerii Martialis Epigrammaton Libri*, Leipzig 1886.)

[18] So Horace, *Serm.* 1. 16 and passim, and Juvenal most obviously in Satire 3.

[19] Even Tacitus, when he longs for the unspoiled virtues of races such as the Germans, takes care to point out that, although their morals are pure, the Germans are idle and do not like to work—and no one would go to Germany, unless mad (*Germ.* 2). Such ambivalence is characteristic of ancient writers when they speak of primitive conditions.

[20] Before we embark on a detailed examination of the *Silvae*, it must be pointed out that we shall probably never be entirely certain whether it was Statius or Pliny the Younger who first devoted his efforts to the praise of the tectonic and technical marvels of civilization. Yet there is considerable likelihood that Pliny was in this matter influenced by Statius. See Hermann Peter, *Der Brief in der römischen Literatur,*

The greater part of the *Silvae* consists of poems extolling man's capacity for performing miracles of skill. In a sense, all of the *Silvae* are poems of glorification.[21] We are, however, chiefly concerned

*Abhandlungen der Kgl.-Sächs. Gesell. der Wiss., Philolog.-Hist. Klasse*, XX 3 (1903), 114-6. According to Peter, Statius was the first to treat in verse the literary theme of *egressus*, digression, which before his time belonged to prose, and specifically to oratory; and that Pliny depended on him. Already before Peter, Friedrich Vollmer in his edition of the *Silvae* (Leipzig 1898), 26, recognized that Statius was the first to make description (*ekphrasis*) a special type of poetry. (I am indebted to Vollmer for his notes on *loci similes* shared by Statius and some of his predecessors and imitators.) Of the more recent critics, Anne-Marie Guillemin, "Les descriptions de villas de Pline le Jeune," *Bulletin de l'Association Guillaume Budé*, XIX (1928), 10, also thinks that Pliny adapted to prose the procedures of contemporary poetry, chiefly that of Statius and Martial (Madame Guillemin points out that *Silvae* 2 appeared before 95 A. D., Martial 4 no later than 96, and Pliny 2 about 97-100), and that in so doing Pliny followed the contemporary canons of politeness. P. 8, she observes how novel is the absence of moralization in Statius', Martial's, and Pliny's descriptions, which exist for their own sake, rather than as an excuse for the insertion of moral judgments. See also A. N. Sherwin-White, *The Letters of Pliny, A Historical and Social Commentary* (Oxford 1966), 186-7, on the dependence of Pliny on Statius. While granting that Pliny took from Statius certain themes, Sherwin-White holds that "the differences far outweigh the resemblances overstressed by Guillemin" (in her notes to Pliny, *Pline le Jeune, Lettres*, Paris, Budé, 1927-47).

Description had been common in both prose and poetry before Statius, and a particular kind of description, that of the so-called *locus amoenus* (in connection with which, see E. R. Curtius, *Europäische Literatur und lateinisches Mittelalter*, 7th ed., Bern 1969, pp. 202-6, and the article of H. Mac L. Currie, "Locus amoenus," *Comp. Lit.* XII, 1960, 94-5, which contains a slight correction to Curtius), also has been part of literature since time immemorial (one recollects *Odyssey* 13. 102-12 and similar passages). Statius, however, describes not just lovely spots, but such as have been made lovelier by the civilizing arts of architecture and engineering, and then still more attractive by the joy and delight of the poet. (See the observant comments of C. P. Segal, "Nature and the World of Man in Greek Literature," *Arion* II 1, 1963, esp. 45-6 and 50-1, on how the Romans of the Empire enjoyed their nature as "part of an enclosed, controlled architectural framework which shuts out the real landscape and replaces it with one that is man-made.")

Statius and Martial frequently write about the same buildings or the same works of art belonging to a rich patron whom they share. It is important, however, to observe that Martial's poems of this kind are not as long and elaborate as those of Statius, and usually lack the feelings of awe and enthusiasm on the part of the spectator-poet, which find full expression in the *Silvae*. Martial's poems on such subjects are concise, catalogue-like descriptions (this is not to deny their attractiveness), while Statius' are really (as has been made clear by Cancik) lyric poems of a novel type. In this lyric quality lies their originality.

Martial's poems in praise of villas, baths, and the like, find few followers later on, while the followers of Statius in the field of descriptive, optimistic lyric are relatively numerous. One reason for such imitation of Statius' descriptions but not Martial's may lie in the hexameter form of most of Statius' poems. When literary skills declined in the late Empire, would-be poets usually turned to the easier meters. Another reason must lie in the fullness of the *Silvae*, which provided the later poets with plentiful material for direct borrowing as well as paraphrase.

[21] Such are the numerous *epicedia* among them, for instance, *Silv.* 3. 3 or 5. 1; the

with Statius' praises of the setting in which his contemporaries disport themselves: a setting in which nature is no longer natural but changed into something artificial and artistic.[22]

poem celebrating Lucan's birthday, 2. 7; the epithalamium, 1. 2; the poems in praise of a youthful favorite's hair, 3. 4, the consulship of the Emperor, 4. 1, or his largesse, 1. 6 and 4. 2. Even poems of congratulation (1. 4, 4. 7 and 8) and a *propempticon* (3. 2) serve this purpose. So does 4. 9, a jesting reproach to Plotius Grypus that he, in return for a copy of Statius' poems, has given him a poor present. This poem gives Statius an opportunity to assert the value of his own poems.

[22] Control over nature seems greatly to have been desired by the Romans of the Empire, and has found expression not in literature alone but in visual arts as well. Roman painting (if one can call Campanian painting Roman—it may have been Greek) at this time invents landscape, and landscape of a particularly civilized type, which delights in depicting elaborate architectural settings in combination with cultivated, well-arranged gardens, in which nature appears thoroughly subdued by man, planned for his comfort, and frequently further embellished by architectural devices such as columns or arches. See Sir Mortimer Wheeler, *Roman Art and Architecture* (New York 1964), 201:

> It may be averred that the Roman delight in the natural vista is properly extended to the architectural vista, and particularly to the architectural interior, in which the Roman mind took a particular and fruitful interest.

K. Woksch, *Der römische Lustgarten, ein Beitrag zur Untersuchung über den Natursinn der Römer*, cited by Biese, 203, holds that the Roman garden imitated the horticulture of Western Asia and was thoroughly subjugated to architectural considerations. On the interpenetration of architecture and the garden, see also Cancik, esp. 45 and 78; "Landschaftsmalerei," *PW* 12. 1. 623; and Pierre Grimal, *Les jardins Romains à la fin de la république et aux deux premiers siècles de l'empire* (Paris 1943). The latter work is indispensable and contains much of interest on Roman aesthetics, but it makes relatively few references to the poets. P. 439, Grimal explains why he considers the evidence of the poets unsatisfactory for his purposes.

Pliny the Elder, 35. 116, attributes the invention of landscape to a certain Ludius (or Tadius, or Studius—the text is unclear at this point) in the age of *divus Augustus*, and calls this genre of painting *amoenissima*. He implies that landscape was confined to murals, rather than easel paintings. Apparently views of natural settings were prized chiefly because of their *trompe d'œil* qualities: in an artificial but perfect form, the outdoors was brought into the house. (See Grimal 213-376.) While gazing at a landscape mural, one could enjoy the illusion that the wall did not exist and that the garden scene was real—the more so because plant and other "natural" motifs abounded on Roman columns and among the decorations along the walls. (Cf. the Elder Pliny's admiring comments in 36. 184 on the famous *asaroton oecon* of Sosus, and Eugénie Sellers Strong, *Roman Sculpture from Augustus to Constantine*, London 1907, 76:

> ... plants appear in Greek art only to be conventionalized into architectural forms; in Roman art the love of natural form conquers the stylistic tendency. To those who are familiar with the conventional forms of the lotus in Egyptian art or of the acanthus in Greek art, it is almost a surprise that even the political Imperial plants, the symbolic laurel, the oak, and the olive, were never conventionalized, but showered their shapely leaves and fruit over every space artistically available.)

Man can create natural settings where one could scarcely expect to find them. (Vitruvius, while he favors the realism of landscape painting, 6. 5. 2, yet disapproves of *trompe d'œil* effects when these are carried to an extreme, as when, 6. 5. 3-4, *pro*

7

The first poem of the collection deals with a huge equestrian statue of Domitian and sets the tone for the *Silvae* that follow.[23] It not only introduces the other poems to the attention of the most powerful and profitable patron of all, the Emperor, but also tells the reader what to expect further in the book: miracles of contemporary civilization in a context of peace and harmony between man and nature. Never has there been a statue to equal that of Domitian:

> Nunc age Fama prior notum per saecula nomen
> Dardanii miretur equi...
> Hunc neque discissis cepissent Pergama muris
> nec grege permixto pueri innuptaeque puellae
> ipse nec Aeneas nec magnus duceret Hector (1. 1. 8-9, 11-3).

Domitian's age is capable of producing works such as were never seen before (100-4), and what is more, these works are particularly attractive because they bear a message of peace:

> Adde quod ille nocens saevosque amplexus Achivos,
> hunc mitis commendat eques: iuvat ora tueri
> mixta notis belli placidamque gerentia pacem (14-6).

*columnis... statuuntur calami... haec autem nec sunt nec fieri possunt nec fuerunt.* Yet he attests the predilection of his contemporaries for such *monstra*, as he calls them: *quemadmodum enim potest calamus vere sustinere tectum?.. at haec falsa videntes homines non reprehendunt sed delectantur.*—On the apparent contradiction between the elder Pliny's and Vitruvius' passages on landscape painting, see Schefold, 79-80.)

The imperial craze for building seems to go along with the notion that man, especially at contemporary Rome, can bring about marvels undreamed of before. Pliny the Elder, 36. 123, says that there has never in the whole world been anything more noteworthy than the Roman aqueducts. Even Frontinus, whose *De aquis* is a dry technical work, occasionally allows himself to express his enthusiasm for the subject:

> Tot aquarum tam multis necessariis molibus pyramidas videlicet otiosas compares
> aut cetera inertia sed fama celebrata opera Graecorum (1. 16).

And in 2. 88 he lauds the aqueducts as dispensers of health and comfort. Civilization to him is a great benefit and joy. (See H. V. Canter, "Praise of Italy in Classical Authors" II, *CJ* 34, 1939, 406-9, on Pliny's, Cassiodorus', and Rutilius' praise of aqueducts, as well as the praise of the other structures of Rome; and contrast with Frontinus' attitude the comment of Fronto, MS Ambr. 75.)

A similar attitude pervades the *Silvae*. Statius must have known contemporary painting, for his wealthy patrons indulged a strong liking for the visual arts. He may have felt the incentive to create similar landscapes in verse. (See H. R. Fairclough, *Love of Nature among the Greeks and Romans*, New York rpr. 1963, 241.) But whether or not he was directly dependent on mural painting, his enthusiasm for *trompe d'œil* effects, for elaborate gardening and interior decoration, and for good plumbing fit well the interests and preoccupations of his epoch.

[23] Statius, no doubt, initially meant it to head Book I only, but as he published additional books of the *Silvae*, this poem came to occupy a prefatory position to the whole collection.

In the other poems of the collection as well, we encounter this theme of civilized peace. Our attention is drawn to the miraculous harmony prevailing between man and beast in the reign of Domitian.[24] Two of the *Silvae* devote great interest to tame animals and their place in human society. A tame lion (2. 5)[25] ends its life gently yet bravely, almost like a man, in that place especially characteristic of Roman civilized life — the arena:

> At non te primo fusum novus obruit ictu
> ille pudor: mansere animi, virtusque cadenti
> a media iam morte redit, nec protinus omnes
> terga dedere minae. Sicut sibi conscius alti
> vulneris adversum moriens it miles in hostem . . .
> sic piger ille gradu solitoque exutus honore
> firmat hians oculos animamque hostemque requirit . . .
> . . . te maesti populusque patresque,
> ceu notus caderes tristi gladiator harena,
> ingemuere mori; magni quod Caesaris ora . . .
> unius amissi tetigit iactura leonis (2. 5. 16-23, 25-7, 30).

Statius' purpose in this poem probably went beyond the mixture of sentimentality and cruelty which here repels the modern reader. For Statius the slaughter of the lion before the eyes of Domitian is justified by the lion's own behavior: he does his job conscientiously and properly, as during his life he used to do the best he could to aid a more humble master:

> . . . abire domo rursusque in claustra reverti
> suetus et a capta iam sponte recedere praeda
> insertasque manus laxo dimittere morsu (4-6).

Like some Stoic, the lion in life and death fulfills his duty toward man.

The parrot of Atedius Melior (2. 4) is another case in point.[26] A spoiled favorite, *domini facunda voluptas* (line 1), he used to greet his master's friends in well-chosen words (*adfatus . . . meditataque verba reddideras,* 7-8), share his banquets (4-7), and live in a marvel of construction, a cage of silver and ivory, whose gates it would open with its beak (11-3).[27] How much more civilized can a bird become? Ancient literature seldom expresses delight in wild creatures living in the

---

[24] We are reminded of the paradisal conditions presaged in Virgil's *Ecl.* 4.

[25] This subject also appears in Martial 1. 6, 14, 22, 48, and elsewhere.

[26] The subject is similar to that of Ovid's *Amores* 2. 6. See also Pliny the Elder *H. N.* 10. 117.

[27] I think such is the meaning.

wilderness,[28] but in Statius' *Silvae*, animal pets are accepted into the context of civilized life as they had never been before. They are presented in human terms, the more effectively to glorify the Golden Age that has become a reality under Domitian.

Not beasts or birds alone, even plants render man's abode more attractive—but do so unnaturally, if prettily. In *Silv.* 2. 3 we read the description of a tree, also belonging to Atedius Melior, and prized for its contorted shape:

> . . .robore ab imo
> incurvata vadis redit inde cacumine recto
> ardua, ceu mediis iterum nascatur ab undis
> atque habitet vitreum tacitis radicibus amnem (2-5).

Statius invents an interesting aetiological story to explain why the tree is crooked. By building a myth around it, he bestows a religious significance upon the tree, thus sanctioning Melior's fondness for its unnatural and contrived beauty; in other words, for those of its features in which it least resembled a tree.[29]

Similar values find expression when Statius describes human dwellings, even when he does so in poems whose proper topic is not architecture or the adaptation of nature to human purposes. In his Epithalamium, *Silv.* 1. 2, Statius does not neglect the opportunity to praise the beauty of the bride's house:

> Hic Libycus Phrygiusque silex, hic dura Laconum
> saxa virent, hic flexus onyx et concolor alto
> vena mari rupesque nitent, quis purpura saepe
> Oebalis et Tyrii moderator livet aeni.
> Pendent innumeris fastigia nixa columnis,
> robora Dalmatico lucent satiata metallo.
> Excludunt radios silvis demissa vetustis
> frigora, perspicui vivunt in marmore fontes.
> Nec servat natura vices; hic Sirius alget,
> bruma tepet versumque domus sibi temperat annum (148-57).

As we see, toward the end of the description the poet singles out the observation that in Violentilla's palace the normal order of nature is

---

[28] Some of the choral passages of Euripides' *Bacchae* may form an exception, as may some Virgilian lines, such as *G.* 1. 379-80 or 383-9.

[29] Grimal, 326-7, explains this poem as an attempt to ennoble the garden of a rich Roman by converting it into an "Arcadia." On Arcadia as a poetic concept, see Bruno Snell, *Die Entdeckung des Geistes*, 3rd ed. (Hamburg 1955), 371-400.

*not* observed. The facilities for cooling or heating the building[30] are as commendable as is the aesthetic pleasure afforded by the luxurious marble which occurs here in such variety and abundance.[31] Simplicity has no place here.[32]

In *Silv*. 1. 6, Statius expresses his pleasure in the elaborate and unusual foods from all the parts of the world, foods offered by the Emperor to those celebrating the Saturnalia. The delicacies become available at the mere bidding of the godlike ruler:

I nunc saecula compara, Vetustas,
antiqui Iovis aureumque tempus:
non sic libera vina tunc fluebant
nec tardum seges occupabat annum (1. 6. 39-42).

Not even Jupiter was able to do better for his subjects during the Golden Age, for then, we are told, harvest came at the appointed season. Now it anticipates its usual time—another departure from nature.

In *Silv*. 3. 4. 47-9 it is Domitian's craze for building that makes him divine:

...Latii montes veterisque Penates
Evandri, quos mole nova pater inclitus orbis
excolit et summis aequat Germanicus astris.

And in 3. 3. 99-103 Statius speaks of the honorable task of Claudius Etruscus, who supervises the expenditures for the imperial buildings:

[evolvit].. quid templa, quid alti
undarum cursus, quid propugnacula poscant
aequoris aut longe series porrecta viarum;
quod domini celsis niteat laquearibus aurum...

Even when dealing with his own circumstances, which cannot have permitted extravagance, Statius gives way to his admiration for grand architecture. While persuading his wife to part from Rome, Statius does not stop at lauding the natural attractions of Naples, such as its glorious climate, its peacefulness and quiet, but adds:

---

[30] Vitruvius 6. 1 explains how and why climate influences the construction of private houses.

[31] Statius likes to describe marble and other building materials, not in their natural state, of course, but worked into the magnificent setting of palatial edifices. In addition to the present passage, see *Silv*. 1. 3. 36, 1. 5. 12 and 34-41 (cf. J. H. Mozley, *Statius*, I, Harvard 1955, Loeb, p. 61, n. d), 3. 1. 5, and others.

[32] On occasion, Statius speaks favorably of simplicity. In *Silv*. 1. 4. 130-1, he remarks that the modest sacrifice of the poor man can please the gods just as well or better than an elaborate offering. But simplicity in performing religious rites is a different matter from simplicity in one's everyday life.

> ....magnificas species cultusque locorum
> templaque et innumeris spatia interstincta columnis,
> et geminam molem nudi tectique theatri ... (3. 5. 89-91)[33]

To see even better how Statius attempts to picture contemporary life as happy, comfortable, and characterized by a refined and harmonious relationship with subjugated nature, let us now turn to those *Silvae* which deal specifically with the marvels brought about by Roman architecture and engineering. We shall see how for the poet these skills become a source of unending delight as he pictures them subduing nature in order to improve it for man's use.

> ...Coquitur pars humida terrae
> protectura hiemes atque exclusura pruinas,
> indomitusque silex curva fornace liquescit (3. 1. 120-2),[34]

he says in celebration of the building of a temple to Hercules in a desolate and barren spot where

> ...steriles ... nuper harenas,
> adsparsum pelago montis latus hirtaque dumis
> saxa nec ulla pati faciles vestigia terras
> cernere erat ... (12-5)

Hercules, whose old, neglected shrine has for a long time occupied this spot, apparently rested content with it in the past, until he noted what Pollius Felix had accomplished nearby in erecting a superb dwelling for himself. Thereupon Hercules became eager to benefit from the modern skills at Pollius' command. Blushing at his poverty, he spoke to Pollius:[35]

---

[33] In 4. 5. 1-28 he speaks of his own wishes as modest: he will be content with a limited sustenance, poor but happy amidst natural surroundings such as trees (not crooked, as far as we know) and the *questus inexpertumque carmen* (line 11) of birds. But this passage is exceptional.—In 5. 1. 121-6 he praises thrifty housewifely virtues, but at line 127 he stops himself by saying *parva loquor* and becomes more grandiloquent.

[34] Virgil *A*. 8. 446 has the words *fornace liquescit*, but he is speaking about Vulcan working in his forge. In Statius' poem, man, not a god, is the heroic worker, resembling Hercules, the mortal who achieved divine status, and who also struggled with dangerous and useless wild things (*vertis in usum / lustra habitata feris*, 168-9). Man is abetted by Hercules, whose temple he is building, but the divine hero's participation is a mythological embellishment not indispensable to the poem.

[35] It is remarkable that, on the mythological level of the poem, Hercules himself asks Pollius for a temple. On the level of reality, Pollius wants a larger building to accommodate his picnic excursions (68-88). A venerable religious cult serves here the convenience of Pollius' leisure hours. The passage furnishes a striking illustration of the value put on comfort by men like Pollius and Statius.

> ....Quid enim ista domus, quid terra, priusquam
> te gauderet, erant? Longo tu tramite nudos   *erat ( aut. erum)*
> texisti scopulos, fueratque ubi semita tantum
> nunc tibi distinctis stat porticus alta columnis,
> ne sorderet iter. Curvi tu litoris ora
> clausisti calidas gemina testudine Nymphas.
> Vix opera enumerem ... (96-102)

Once the work is afoot, Hercules is willing to lend his enormous strength to tasks such as breaking rock too solid to be split by steel, yet he seems to lack the essential architectural expertise, which is, however, fully within the grasp of a modern Roman such as Pollius. In Hercules' remote time, extraordinary work presumably was accomplished by magic, not technology, and the poet appropriately asks if, perhaps, such magic has been active here:

> ...Tyrione haec moenia plectro
> an Getica venere lyra?.. (16-7)

Yet this is only a rhetorical question, which Statius leaves unanswered. In another poem, *Silv.* 2. 2, in which the possessions of Pollius Felix himself find eloquent praise, we learn that a builder such as he has no mythological wizardry at his command but does just as well without it:

> Iam Methymnaei vatis manus et chelys una
> Thebais et Getici cedat tibi gloria plectri:
> et tu saxa moves, et te nemora alta sequuntur (60-2).[36]

How splendidly indeed is Pollius lodged! Nature has provided a good location for his villa (2. 2. 15-6, 26-9), but that is all that she has done. It was up to him to better for his comfort this secluded and peaceful spot. The wilderness of rough rocks was urbanized for civilized promenades:

> Inde per obliquas erepit porticus arces,
> urbis opus, longoque domat saxa aspera dorso.
> Qua prius obscuro permixti pulvere soles
> et feritas inamoena viae, nunc ire voluptas (30-3).

The attractiveness of Pollius' country retreat lies in the way it combines the charms of nature and the best comforts of city life.[37]

---

[36] In lines 112-20 we learn that Pollius' poetry is so good that it can work the usual poet's magic of controlling dolphins, and even Sirens, but in the present passage, when he is constructing a building, Pollius achieves practical ends by practical means.

[37] The phrase *urbis opus* is in use before Statius: see Virgil *A.* 5. 118 and Ovid *Fasti* 6. 641.

These are, in fact, inseparable:

> . . .locine
> ingenium an domini mirer prius? (44-5)

ponders the poet, and then enumerates the various features of this union of nature and human skill. The following passage deserves to be quoted in full:

> . . .Haec domus ortus
> aspicit et Phoebi tenerum iubar, illa cadentem
> detinet exactamque negat dimittere lucem,
> cum iam fessa dies et in aequora montis opaci
> umbra cadit vitreoque natant praetoria ponto.
> Haec pelagi clamore fremunt, haec tecta sonoros
> ignorant fluctus terraeque silentia malunt.
> His favit natura locis, hic victa colenti
> cessit et ignotos docilis mansuevit in usus.
> Mons erat hic, ubi plana vides, et lustra fuerunt,
> quae nunc tecta subis; ubi nunc nemora ardua cernis,
> hic nec terra fuit. Domuit possessor et illum
> formantem rupes expugnantemque secuta
> gaudet humus. Nunc cerne iugum discentia saxa
> intrantesque domos iussumque recedere montem (45-59).

We observe that throughout these lines the poet not only emphasizes that nature has been mastered by intelligence and skill,[38] but delights as well in the capricious and playful selectivity which Pollius is free to exercise. Indeed, the lord of this skilfully designed villa seems to have nature herself at his command: if he wishes, he can have his windows admit the morning, or else the setting, sun.[39] If the fancy strikes him, he can so choose his apartments that he will either be able to enjoy the sound of the sea or else do entirely without it—and all this in the same house. Pollius has done away with a hill and has planted trees where none grew before, yet still other spots he has left as they used to be. Now he can enjoy nature both in her pristine and her subdued state (52-3), although the latter seems to be the better and more admirable condition. At least, Statius dwells on it at greater length and says that nature willingly gave in to her master (53-4, 58). Most of the estate has experienced a change so great that Statius' lines remind the reader of those catalogues of impossibilities (*adynata*) that in previous poetry suggested not a real world but one turned topsy-turvy. Here, however, fancy has become reality.

---

[38] Or *ingenium*, on which see Vollmer's note to *Silv.* 1. 3. 15.

[39] See Vitruvius 6. 4 on the desirable exposure of a house to light and sun.

The passage quoted above does not exhaust the pleasures available to Pollius. Lines 63-72 tell of his varied and rich art collection. In lines 72-85 Statius shifts attention from the joy of viewing works of art inside the house to the charms of gazing through the windows at the natural surroundings of the villa. Once more we are made aware of a balance between the delights of nature and of art, both of them at Pollius' beck and call. We are told that the windows of the villa are arranged in such a manner that from each room one can have a view of a completely different character — a seeming impossibility of the reality of which, however, Statius assures us. The differences among these vistas are brought out by Statius' choice of proper names to attach to them. These are, no doubt, names of actually existing places, but Statius probably uses them poetically for their adjectival connotations as well. Inarime may well have suggested *inanis* to a Roman reader, especially if there was an active volcano periodically laying waste the island so named.[40] Prochyta would seem to stand for[41] a piece of land extending out into the sea[42] and probably washed over by the sea waves.[43] Mythological interest is directly suggested by *armiger Hectoris*, a phrase which Statius, for the sake of variety, prefers to the place name in actual use, Misenum.[44] From one window Pollius can see where lies *pelago circumflua Nesis*; from another, Euploea, and *quae ferit curvos exserta Megalia fluctus*. Both of these bear names suggesting their natural features. The cheerful name of Limon follows them, and then the list ends in a reference to Naples herself.[45] This catalogue of attractions flows into still another, an enumeration (85-94) of the different kinds of marble that decorate the loftiest chamber of the villa. Statius takes the opportunity to mention the country of origin of each, skilfully and subtly extending the range of beautiful spots over which Pollius' fancy can roam. From the islands and promontories visible directly from the windows of the villa, our attention thus shifts to such fabulous parts of the world as Syene or

---

[40] Cf. Virgil *A.* 9. 716.

[41] Notwithstanding Dionysius' of Halicarnassus (1. 53. 3) statement that it was named for Aeneas' nurse. See also *Aeneid* 7. 715.

[42] See the reference to Philo Mechanicus in Liddell-Scott-Jones under προχέω.

[43] Statius characterizes Prochyta as *aspera*.

[44] Prose authors, such as Pliny the Younger, *Epist.* 6. 16. 20, use this name.

[45] A similar list of almost all the same places appears in 3. 1. 147-53, but there the function of the catalogue is different. It does not excite the imagination but, by stating which places in the vicinity will participate in the games newly established in honor of Hercules, serves to emphasize the god's importance.

Numidia, as well as several Greek lands. And all along we are kept aware of both art and nature, as well as the tenuous distinction between the two. For instance, when we read that the marble of Amyclae *molles imitatur rupibus herbas* (line 91), we recognize that the marble used for decorating this splendid chamber is a natural product, yet we learn that even in its natural coloration it imitates something else in nature—grass. Indoors, at Pollius' villa, this Amyclaean marble serves as a reminder of the grass outside, just as the Carystian marble (line 93) reminds one of water.[46]

Pollius' villa has many notable features besides the living quarters. Foremost among them are his splendid baths:

> Gratia prima loci, gemina testudine fumant
> balnea et e terris occurrit dulcis amaro
> Nympha mari. Levis hic Phorci chorus udaque crines
> Cymodoce viridisque cupit Galatea lavari (17-20).[47]

Here is a great improvement on the natural facilities available to the Nymphs and other creatures of the sea bitter with salt—they would be happy to bathe here (18-20).[48] Even Hercules, as we remember (*Silv.* 3. 1. 100), took note of these baths. Yet Pollius is not the only one of Statius' patrons who has such wonderful plumbing at his disposal. Another rich man, Manilius Vopiscus, possesses baths no less splendid. When Statius speaks of these, he again couches his description in the form of a catalogue of impossibilities:

> ...An [canam] quae graminea suscepta crepidine fumant
> balnea et impositum ripis algentibus ignem,
> quaque vaporiferis iunctus fornacibus amnis
> ridet anhelantes vicino flumine Nymphas? (1. 3. 43-6)

A grass-grown slope and smoke; icy cold and fire; steaming

---

[46] Just how it does so is not clear. See, however, Phillimore's view, quoted by D. A. Slater in his translation of the *Silvae* (Oxford 1908), and then quoted in turn by Mozley *ad locum*, that when one sees the marble one is reminded of the sea near which the Carystian quarries lie.

[47] I am inclined to take the phrase *gratia prima loci* with what follows, as does Mozley, rather than with the preceding sentence, as does Vollmer, because I think that Statius formally begins his description of the buildings with these words.

[48] For lines 15-20 Statius seems to borrow some phrases from *Aeneid* 1. 166 and 5. 822-6. Of the Virgilian passages which he echoes the first is concerned with an exceptionally uncivilized region, while the second describes sea divinities as they accompany a divine master, Neptune, in a wild flight over the waves. What he has found in Virgil, Statius uses in a totally different context. He suggests that the Nymphs and the sea beasts long for the comforts of civilization which, however, are unavailable to them. The Virgilian echoes emphasize the wildness of these creatures.

furnaces and a stream—this list of contrasts ends with the incongruous but effective picture of Nymphs caught breathless in an unexpected cloud of steam, while the stream laughs at them. Harnessed by civilization, the stream seems to feel superior to the naïve Nymphs unfamiliar with such contemporary marvels as Manilius' baths.[49]

Nor are these the only miracles worked by plumbing at Manilius' villa. All the bedchambers have running water—a luxury the poet commends no less than the beautiful and expensive decorations of these rooms:

Quid primum mediumve canam, quo fine quiescam?
Auratasne trabes an Mauros undique postes
an picturata lucentia marmora vena
mirer, an emissas per cuncta cubilia Nymphas? (34-7)[50]

An elaborate system of decorative pools and fountains near which one can picnic is supplemented by the proximity of the Aqua Marcia (64-7). The aqueduct finds extravagant praise at the expense of the legendary haunts of water divinities. Anio himself is happier in the aqueduct than in his own habitat, and so would be a great number of other gods of streams and woodland, if they had the opportunity (68-89). What is more, the proximity of the Anio has been used at this villa in such a way that the dwelling lies partly on one bank, partly on the other. Nature is here taken indoors. Just as a portion of the building has been erected around an old tree, allowing it to rear its head up above the roof (59-61), so the stream too finds itself in the middle of Manilius' dwelling, between the two halves of the house placed on the opposite banks (2-4, 24-6). The inhabitants of the villa see one another and talk across the stream, and can almost clasp hands over it (30-1).[51] The builder's skill in using nature for human convenience and delectation does not stop here. The nearness of the water has been utilized to condition the climate

---

[49] Grimal, 207, remarks on such luxurious baths placed in a country setting: "C'est ainsi que les citadins aiment ce qui rappelle la campagne, et détestent être privés de leur ville."

[50] The word *Nymphas* in line 37 carries no mythological significance. It is a metonym for water.

[51] Here Statius may be putting to a rather mundane use Lucan's words about Caesar and Pompey confronting each other from opposite military camps (5. 471-2).—Building a house around a tree seems to have been an ancient Germanic custom (see the description of King Volsung's hall in the *Volsunga Saga*), but Manilius probably followed his own, rather than barbarian, predilections.

at the villa so that the summer sun has no power there (5-8).[52]

Nature around Manilius' villa is more richly endowed than it was at that of Pollius:

> Ingenium quam mite solo, quae forma beatis
> ante manus artemque locis! Non largius usquam
> indulsit natura sibi ... (15-7)[53]

Here no hills had to be cut away, no woods planted, only the natural landscape to be utilized to the best advantage of the villa. But Statius points out that man's work here has been lessened by the capacity of nature to achieve a certain amount of artifice without man's help. Indeed, nature furthers Manilius' happiness by using her powers to counterfeit and pretend:

> ...Non largius usquam
> indulsit natura sibi. Nemora alta citatis
> incubuere vadis; fallax responsat imago
> frondibus, et longas eadem fugit umbra per undas.
> Ipse Anien (miranda fides) infraque superque
> saxeus hic tumidam rabiem spumosaque ponit
> murmura, ceu placidi veritus turbare Vopisci
> Pieriosque dies et habentes carmina somnos (16-23).

Reflection and echo, those most impressive instances of imitation in nature, are here present or absent in accord with the comfort of the master of the villa. And when her efforts are surpassed by human skill, nature seems to rejoice in man's success:

> ...splendor ab alto
> defluus et nitidum referentes aera testae
> monstravere solum, varias ubi picta per artes
> gaudet humus superatque novis assarota figuris (53-6).

---

[52] Statius refers to ancient air-conditioning not in this passage only but elsewhere as well. In 1. 2. 154-7 we meet the significant statement:

> Excludunt radios silvis demissa vetustis
> frigora, perspicui vivunt in marmore fontes.
> Nec servat natura vices: hic Sirius alget,
> bruma tepet versumque domus sibi temperat annum.

The emphasis is on man's victory over the natural temper of the seasons.

[53] Codex Matritensis has the reading *arte* in line 16. *Ante* is a conjecture of Bursian. Since Statius in such contexts as this uses the word *ingenium* for human inventiveness, *arte* would seem to be a better reading. The sense of the passage then will be: "What a delicate, inventive touch has been applied to the land; how have these happy spots been shaped by the skill of human hand! Nature herself has never been so indulgent." Such an interpretation leaves, however, unexplained the word *artemque*. If, on the other hand, we accept the reading *ante*, the sense will be that, before art had touched the place, it was already beautiful, therefore how much more beautiful is it now, after it has been shaped in accordance with Manilius' wishes!

*Gaudet humus,* says the poet, choosing a word which suggests not the floor of a human dwelling such as he is describing but the floor of nature, the soil.[54] The line which divides the natural from the artificial becomes so much the more tenuous. We note that even the light enters the room in such a way that it well illuminates the mosaic of the floor—another instance of the builder's cleverness, but also of the cooperation of nature.[55]

In another poem, *Silv.* 1. 5, Statius devotes himself to the encomium not of a whole estate but of one magnificent part of it only: the baths.[56] Here again we read about a profusion of marble (12-3, 34-44). Here too daylight is admitted in a clever and interesting way, to light but not to warm:

> Multus ubique dies, radiis ubi culmina totis
> perforat atque sol improbus uritur aestu (45-6).

The light of the sun is controlled, its heat surpassed. Yet the rival force of fire is also well under control:

> ...Stupet ipse beatas
> circumplexus opes et parcius imperat ignis...
> ...languidus ignis inerrat
> sedibus et tenuem volvunt hypocausta vaporem (43-4, 58-9).

In short, even the baths of Nero are no better (62-3).

Statius calls on the Nymphs to frequent the baths of Claudius Etruscus—an appropriate invocation, since the Nymphs may well stand metonymically for water.[57] But not all Nymphs are invoked: Statius emphatically turns away the uncivilized, wild, dangerous springs such as Salmacis, Cebrenis, and the one into which Hylas fell (20-2). Instead, he invokes the domestic Nymphs of Latium, such as have been channeled into the famous aqueducts:

> Vos mihi, quae Latium septenaque culmina, Nymphae,
> incolitis Thybrimque novis attollitis undis,
> quas praeceps Anien atque exceptura natatus
> Virgo iuvat Marsasque nives et frigora ducens

---

[54] Cf. Lygdamus 3. 3. 16, *aurataeque trabes marmoreumque solum.*

[55] The illusionistic element is very strong throughout *Silv.* 2. 3. The allusion to the famous Asarotos in line 56 contributes to it.

[56] In other poems too we meet passing laudatory references to the miracles of skill involved in building baths. In 5. 3. 169-71, for instance, Statius speaks with admiration of the union of fire and water at Baiae.

[57] Grimal, 454, thinks that Statius is referring to statues of Nymphs. Yet *Silv.* 1. 3. 45 uses the name of Nymphs as a metonym only, as does an epigram ascribed to Felix in the *Anth. Lat.* (Baehrens IV, p. 335), and probably echoing *Silv.* 1. 3. 45.

Marcia, praecelsis quarum vaga molibus unda
crescit et innumero pendens transmittitur arcu:
vestrum opus aggredimur, vestra est, quam carmine molli
pando, domus. Non umquam aliis habitastis in antris
ditius ... (23-31)

In these lines we hear not the poet of nature but the poet of engineering. He extols the Nymphs because they do useful work.

Statius' enthusiasm for civilization finds its most striking expression in *Silv.* 4. 3, a poem dealing with the Via Domitiana. In the Preface to the Fourth Book of the *Silvae*, Statius takes a strictly utilitarian view of this road:

... tertio [opusculo] viam Domitianam miratus sum, qua gravissimam harenarum moram [imperator] exemit.

Another poem of the same Book, 4. 4, also commends, although briefly, the speed with which a letter can travel over good roads (1-5), as well as the wonderful sights (miracles of their builder's skill themselves) to which such a road can lead: Augustus' *stagnum navale* and suburban gardens (6-7), impressive mines (99).[58] Poem 4. 3, however, is exclusively devoted to the praises of a good modern road, and references to other blessings of civilization are here incidental, although when they occur they reinforce the optimistic mood of the piece; indeed, canal-building (7-8) and cultivation of wheat in those spots which formerly did not lend themselves to agriculture (11-2) may have been facilitated by the Via Domitiana. The greater portion of the poem expresses joy at man's successful effort at levelling mountains, cutting down forests,[59] building a firm surface across soft and shifting sands. The river god Vulturnus himself, leaning not against some mossy bank or rock, as would befit a river, but against the huge arch of a Roman bridge (69-70), does not regret his former, natural state[60] but rejoices in being civilized: channeled, bridged, dredged (line 86, *nec sordere sinis*) and used for irrigation (86-7). In short, says he, only now is he beginning to be a proper kind of river (*amnis esse coepi*, 80).

After another series of lines acclaiming the swiftness and comfort of travel on the new road, no lesser figure than the Cumaean Sibyl steps forth to praise this supreme accomplishment and Domitian, who has brought it about. Statius pretends to yield to this greater *vates*

---

[58] Mining serves as a topic for praise also in 1. 1. 42.

[59] This passage is different from the epic use of the theme. In the epic, timber is cut for funeral pyres or for building ships, as in Statius' own *Achilleid* 1. 426-9.

[60] *Pudet*, says he referring to it, line 80.

(119-20). Of course, if the Sibyl herself extols the road, what better witness to its excellence can the reader ask?

> ...sic virgineo profatur ore:
> "Dicebam, veniet — manete campi
> atque amnis — veniet favente caelo,
> qui foedum nemus et putres harenas
> celsis pontibus et via levabit.
> En! hic est deus .. " (123-8)

The natural features of the land are here characterized as unpleasant: *foedum, putres*, but by the grace of the Emperor's command over the fields and the streams, their natural, useless condition finds itself immeasurably improved—and improved for ages and ages. For the poem ends with the prediction that the new road is destined to last as long as Rome.[61]

There is nothing quite like this in the work of Statius' contemporary Martial.[62] When he praises the farm of Julius Martialis as a pleasant and hospitable place (4. 64), his emphasis rests on the charm of the country around the farm and on its rustic hospitality. Some mythological references embellish the poem: not even the garden[63] of the Hesperides is lovelier, says Martial; this villa is as hospitable as the house of Alcinous. He mentions the proximity of the Pons Mulvius as well as the traffic on the river—but does so only to set off better the restful atmosphere of the villa. We are told that here it is quiet even though boats pass close to the house, as do the vehicles crossing the bridge.

In 10. 51 also Martial recalls the ease and placidity of life in the country. The most entertaining lines of this poem speak of lying on a couch and looking from it in different directions. Without changing one's vantage point, one can see on the one side boats sailing the sea, and river boats on the other side (9-10). But, unlike Statius, Martial is

---

[61] The passages and poems discussed here do not include all of Statius' references to the blessings of civilized amenities of life. Almost all of the *Silvae* are permeated by such references. To give an example, *Silv.* 4. 6, a laudatory description of a statuette of Hercules, fits admirably into Statius' view of life as a series of peaceful pleasures experienced in the midst of the creations of human skill (Martial, 9. 43 and 44, describes the same statuette.)

[62] In 4. 49, Martial rejects the thought of writing pastoral poetry. In 12. 18 he speaks of his delight in the real, unadorned countryside. When Martial employs literary conceits, he is full of humor. He cannot treat these conceits as seriously as does Statius.

[63] On Martial's love of gardens, see Grimal 446-8. P. 448, Grimal observes: "... toujours, Martial fait passer la rusticité, même un peu grossière, avant les recherches du luxe."

not concerned with the inventiveness of the builder who has arranged the villa so as to make it possible to enjoy these views from a couch.[64] His emphasis is on blissful indolence, *tunicata quies* (line 6), in surroundings which seem to be altogether natural, not artificially arranged:

> O nemus, o fontes solidumque madentis harenae
> litus et aequoreis splendidus Anxur aquis (7-8).

Urban civilization with its theaters, fora, baths, and temples, is left behind, abandoned to Quirinus:

> Dicere te lassum quotiens ego credo Quirino:
> "Quae tua sunt, tibi habe: quae mea, redde mihi." (15-6)[65]

This is a veritable Cockaigne,[66] as is also the scene pictured in 1. 49. 27, where the neighboring forest runs down the hill right into the furnace.

In another epigram Martial pictures another friend, Apollinaris, lounging on a couch so conveniently that he can fish without rising from his restful position (10. 30. 16-8). Again Martial offers us a picture of absolute, Cockaigne-like comfort, and stresses not modern conveniences but simplicity: the *nomenclator* points out to his master some remarkable fish instead of the clients who usually throng around him in the busy city, and several mythological incidents are mentioned in the poem to make it clear that, when he is staying at his country place, Apollinaris has no desire for any other, even for the haunts of Circe (8).

*Epigram* 12. 31 also lauds country life. It lacks the whimsical character of 10. 51 or 10. 30, but like those poems it too stresses the simple, unsophisticated comforts, such as the abundance of unpretentious but wholesome food:

[64] We are not even told what makes these views possible. Is it an ingenious arrangement of windows in one and the same room? Or has the couch been set up out-of-doors?

[65] A nostalgia for simplicity can also be felt in *Aeneid* 8, in Propertius 4. 1 and 4. 4. 1-14, and in numerous other passages in Latin literature, but there we detect the poets' longing for the good old days. Martial speaks of contemporary conditions.

[66] Such pictures recur from time to time in Latin literature until its last days. Claudian, *In Rufinum* 1. 380-7, describes the future reign of Honorius as a Golden Age. Purple sheep will, of course, be available (how could they be lacking in any paradise after Virgil?), but so will other conveniences readily associated in our mind with the Land of Cockaigne, such as rivers of wine and lakes of oil. It should be profitable and interesting to follow the development of such motifs through the whole of ancient literature.

Hoc nemus, hi fontes, haec textilis umbra supini
palmitis, hoc riguae ductile flumen aquae,
prataque nec bifero cessura rosaria Paesto,
quodque viret Iani mense nec alget holus;
quaeque natat clusis anguilla domestica lymphis,
quaeque gerit similes candida turris aves,
munera sunt dominae: post septima lustra reverso
si mihi Nausicaa patrios concederet hortos,
Alcinoo possem dicere "Malo meos".

Such are Martial's descriptions of the country when he is in a genial mood. In other poems he pays more attention to luxury, but his purpose is then frequently satyrical: at a grand villa where the vegetation is exotic and the baths enormous, and *calcatus ... sub pede lucet onyx* (12. 50. 4),[67] the owner has been so carried away by his pursuit of extravagance that he has forgotten to allow space for the practical demands of life, such as eating and sleeping.

Generally, then, Martial either speaks of the charm of simplicity or else makes fun of unnecessary elaboration in the dwellings of his contemporaries. On occasion, however, he expresses admiration for some grand building. *Epigram* 8. 68 is given to the praise of Entellus' hothouse, productive through the whole year, while 6. 42 deals with the baths of Claudius Etruscus, the same baths which Statius celebrates in *Silv.* 1. 5. This identity of subject recommends a closer look at the poem.

Martial's poem is shorter than Statius'.[68] It begins with a concise but effective and somewhat amusing hyperbole:

Etrusci nisi thermulis lavaris,
illotus morieris, Oppiane.

There follows a brief list of bathing places that cannot compare with the baths of Etruscus. Martial does not include springs or rivers, but likens the baths to similar establishments elsewhere, rather than to anything in nature. Then he concisely mentions the expensive materials used in the construction, and commends the clear water in near-by aqueducts to those who prefer to bathe like Spartans. The poem ends with the repetition of the line *illotus morieris, Oppiane.*[69]

---

[67] We are reminded of the love with which Statius dwells on the exorbitant use of expensive building materials.

[68] 24 lines as compared to 65. Besides, Statius writes in long hexameter lines, Martial in short Phalaeceans, which are not suited to full descriptions. They are more fit for hinting than for expounding. ? St. Silv. IV 3 in 11-54ll.

[69] In his comments on this poem, Friedlaender identifies the watering places

Here we have none of Statius' pictures of rivers pressed into the service of man. Aqueducts are taken for granted, and baths praised without any attempt to interpret their relation to their natural surroundings. Not only is Martial's version of this topic less elaborate but also more humorous: he takes lightly what seems to overwhelm Statius.

A similar difference of approach characterizes *Epigr.* 1. 86. 1-2 and *Silv.* 1. 3. 30-1. Martial's lines are funny and entertaining. The poet jests about the extreme closeness of his living quarters to those of his neighbors: when he leans out of his window, he can practically touch a certain Novius.[70] Statius works the same situation into his description of a great villa, one of the attractions of which lies in the way it spreads on both banks of a river, so that people can reach hands across the water. What in Martial's poem was the jest of a poor man, Statius turns into yet another astounding accomplishment of architecture at the service of the rich.[71]

In still another poem, Martial alludes (so it seems) to the Virgilian purple sheep. He is addressing the city of Corduba:

> ...albi quae superas oves Galaesi
> nullo murice nec cruore mendax,
> sed tinctis gregibus colore vivo (12. 63. 3-5).

Here nature has been surpassed by herself, not by man's skill, and Martial implies that such wool is preferable to that dyed by human hands. Nor does he say, as Statius might under similar circumstances, that nature attempts to serve man by furnishing him with wool already colored. Martial simply is listing the advantages of Corduba, without making of them anything more than a short but attractive catalogue; and it is likely, moreover, that in speaking of his colorful sheep he is being not Virgilian but geographically exact.[72]

---

mentioned and suggests that Statius' poem was probably written later than that of Martial, since it seems to contain a correction of the latter: Martial speaks of onyx and *ophites* used in the baths, while Statius expressly says, line 35, that these kinds of stone were rejected by the builder as unworthy.

[70] Martial may be parodying Ovid *Heroid.* 18. 179-80, the words of Leander to Hero.

[71] Martial's poem probably preceded that of Statius, for which see above. See Schanz-Hosius II 541-2 and 551 for the probable chronology of the *Silvae* and Martial's epigrams.

[72] See Hugo Bluemner, *Die gewerbliche Thätigkeit der Völker des klassischen Alterthums* (Leipzig 1869), 129, n. 1-5. Bluemner refers to Martial 5. 37. 7 and to many other passages in order to demonstrate that the wool of Spanish sheep had a natural yellowish or reddish coloration. Baetic wool especially was known for its reddish

To sum up, then, Martial's approach to the conveniences and luxuries of Roman civilization is quite unlike Statius'. He is not allured by them, as is Statius, and, unlike Statius, has no interest in constructing a coherent picture of the enigmatic interplay between nature and art. Yet he is as fond of comfort as anyone, and accepts modern life with its baths, hothouses, and aqueducts, its circus performances and banquets—so long as he is spared excessive noise and trouble. By looking at the poems of Martial, rival and contemporary of Statius, we can see the unusual qualities of the *Silvae* all the better.

Pliny the Younger is the first to introduce descriptions of skilfully arranged houses and gardens into prose.[73] Usually he values a villa chiefly as a retreat for his studies,[74] and his enthusiasm for this or that country place often takes the form of a catalogue of its advantages.[75] On several occasions, however, when Pliny praises his country estates at greater length, we find him still very much interested in the natural assets of an estate, but also stressing how very well its man-made attractions fit into the natural setting. Much of this attitude is not peculiar to Pliny alone, but to the ancients in general, but Pliny expresses it with particular charm and fullness.[76]

When in *Epist.* 8. 8 he is impressed with the natural beauties of the Clitumnus, he does not omit to mention the temples on its lovely banks. In 5. 6, most of Pliny's interest is devoted to the natural qualities of a Tuscan estate, but his praise of these culminates in the following passage:

> Magnam capies voluptatem, si hunc regionis situm ex monte prospexeris. Neque enim terras tibi, sed formam aliquam ad eximiam pulchritudinem pictam videberis cernere; ea varietate, ea descriptione, quounque inciderint oculi, reficientur (5. 6. 13).

cast.—In *Epigr.* 12. 98. 1-2 and in *Apoph.* 14. 133. 1-2 also Martial speaks of wool which is colorful although it has not been dyed. Juvenal 12. 37-42 seems to make fun of this colorful wool.

[73] He feels that such themes are novel to prose. See *Epist.* 5. 6. 43-4, where he compares his efforts to those of the poets. He probably was the first prosaist to graft descriptions of houses onto the time-honored topic dealing with the *locus amoenus*. See footnote 20.

[74] As in 4. 6, 9. 15, 9. 36, and other letters.

[75] As in 1. 3. 1 or 1. 24. 3.

[76] Pliny's favorable attitude toward the accomplishments of his age is well illustrated by *Epist.* 6. 21. 1: *Sum ego is* (var. *ex iis*) *qui mirer antiquos, non tamen ut quidam temporum nostrorum ingenia despicio.* See also *Epist.* 8. 4. 1-2.

When he says that a view from a hill is as good as a picture, Pliny implies that a picture can contain more beauty than nature. The favorable comparison of a work of art to a work of nature is, of course, commonplace and has been much in use before Pliny,[77] but in his case we may accept such a statement as the programme behind his descriptions of the country.[78] Except perhaps in *Epist.* 8. 20, where he pictures the strangeness of a volcanic lake, he has no love for wild places, and even in that Epistle his interest is more that of a scientist than a lover of nature.[79] A like curiosity about natural phenomena finds expression in 4. 30, where Pliny asks Licinius Sura for an explanation of the mysterious properties of a spring. We note, however, that despite the mystery, the spring has been so managed that it flows into Pliny's own dining room, where the master of the house can enjoy its regular fluctuations as he eats:

> Iuxta recumbis et vesceris atque etiam ex ipso fonte (nam est frigidissimus) potas, interim ille certis dimensisque momentis vel subtrahitur vel adsurgit (3).

Here nature is man's toy. Pliny's indolent attitude toward the spring reminds us of Martial's little poem on the pleasure of fishing from one's couch. As a matter of fact, Pliny too can enjoy a similar convenience from the terrace of a villa:

> ... possis ... piscari hamumque de cubiculo ac paene etiam de lectulo ut e navicula iacere (9. 7. 4).

Nature subdued, dressed, and adapted to man's pleasure and convenience is the kind of nature that Pliny likes. Luxury he regards as unimportant, but ease and comfort he values above all. Even before beginning the description of a villa in 2. 17, he is careful to note that this villa is easier to reach on horseback than in a carriage. It is

> ... usibus capax, non sumptuosa tutela (3) ... atrium frugi nec tamen sordidum... parvula sed festiva area (4) ... cellae elegantes quam sumptuosae (11)...[80]

---

[77] The myth of Pygmalion comes to mind.

[78] See Biese 162-7 on Pliny's fondness for civilized nature.

[79] Infrequently he grants that some natural wonder cannot be improved by man, for instance, in 5. 6. 7. Behind such admissions we feel the conviction that on most occasions nature can, indeed, be improved upon.

[80] On the construction and arrangement of these villas, see the notes of Madame Guillemin, *Pline le Jeune, Lettres,* as well as the notes of Sherwin-White, who is somewhat distrustful of her findings. Her note 3 on *Epist.* 5. 6. 40 summarizes what she regards as the essential features of ancient (it might be more appropriate to say, Roman imperial) love of nature.

Throughout this Epistle, the important theme is comfort achieved by ingenuity. Several subordinate themes follow one another as Pliny leads the reader from one part of the villa to the next, until by the end of the letter he has covered the whole grounds. He writes in turn about the effective cooling and heating of the house and grounds, the lighting and sound-proofing of the rooms, and the utilization of the best possibilities for beautiful views. All these accoutrements of civilized life are full of artifice, but not artifice alone: what strikes in their description is not the power of the architect's or the engineer's tools—a power divorced from nature—but the builder's cleverness, his ability to take advantage of the various natural features of the estate in such a way that nature is here preserved for enjoyment, but does not remain in the rough. Instead, it has been polished and improved. Not being a poet, Pliny, unlike Statius, does not speak of Nymphs longing for civilization, but his point of view is similar to that of the *Silvae*: the sun and the sea, the winds and the shade can be utilized for an easier and more comfortable life, if only one possesses the technical knowledge necessary for manipulating such natural forces.[81]

Thus, we find, a number of architectural tricks has been employed to outwit the weather. A portico at Pliny's villa is

> egregium... adversus tempestates receptaculum; nam specularibus ac multo magis imminentibus tectis muniuntur (4).

Elsewhere,

> includitur angulus, qui purissimum solem continet et accendit... Ibi omnes silent venti exceptis qui nubilum inducunt et serenum ante quam usum loci eripiunt... (7)

This *hibernaculum*, as Pliny calls it, puts to good advantage the heating power of the sun, and we may assume that the sun does a good job of lighting it as well. By saying that winds are quiet and do not disturb the peaceful silence of the *hibernaculum*, Pliny introduces the theme of soundproofing, which will recur as the Epistle progresses.

Next to the *hibernaculum* is a *cubiculum*, "*quod ambitum solis fenestris omnibus sequitur*" (8). As in the previous passage Pliny mentioned the usefulness of the sun as a source of heat, so here we learn of the pleasant way in which the sun's light has been

---

[81] Pliny is not the inventor of this view, only an innovator in its literary treatment. See Madame Guillemin's note on *Epist.* 4. 30, where she points to the Roman predilection for dining near a spring or a fountain. Also read her notes to 5. 6. 24 and 5. 6. 32, on the nature of Roman gardens.

utilized in the *cubiculum*, which contains a collection of books and is reserved for assiduous reading (*non legendos libros sed lectitandos*).

Soon we pass into a room which is brilliantly lighted not only by the sun but also by waves reflecting sunlight (10). Later in the essay, when Pliny describes the garden attached to his villa, he seeks to make the reader aware of the variety of the plantings and the views opening from the house: a predictable way to talk of a garden. In the present passage, however, he is just as much concerned with diversity, only here it is the diversity of technological accomplishments that interests him: the ways in which the house is heated, cooled, and lighted. He is particularly interested in the use of the natural heat of the sun, but mentions artificial heat too, and points to its ingenuity:

> Adhaeret dormitorium membrum transitu interiacente, qui suspensus et tubulatus conceptum vaporem salubri temperamento huc illuc digerit et ministrat (9).

The next apartment to which we pass strikes us by a still different kind of inventiveness:

> ... cubiculum cum procoetone, altitudine aestivum, munimentis hibernum; est enim subductum omnibus ventis (10).

The description continues in a similar vein. It is hardly necessary to mention all the other rooms which our author commends because they lie cleverly exposed to the sun or sheltered from wind. The latter convenience affords him extraordinary pleasure when it can be controlled by closing or opening windows on one or the other side of a corridor (16, 19). Even in the garden is the sun used with noteworthy skill: a bed of violets is screened from the wind by the *cryptoporticus*, but at the same time is warmed by the reflection of the sun from the walls[82] of this marvellous corridor (17), which on other occasions (18) performs an opposite, complementary, duty by casting shade on a portion of the grounds.

The sea has been allowed to creep right up to one of the dining rooms (5), probably for the sake of the view it affords. Still another dining room is quite secure from the noise of the sea, even during a storm (13). Finally (22-3), a bed-chamber is soundproofed by an air cushion in the form of a corridor. Light too can be almost completely excluded from this room when the windows are closed. Not ordinary noise only but even the sound of the sea and the storm can be kept

---

[82] And possibly also windows? Window glass is attested by Pompeiian excavations.

out of this room, along with daylight and even flashes of lightning. Since the sun is not used here for its heat, a *hypocauston* is put to work, while the beauty of a sunrise can still be enjoyed from an adjoining room.

Pliny delights in all these conveniences not only because he vividly realizes that they are at his disposal but perhaps even more so because various technical problems at his villa have found solutions of such charm and variety. The sun, the wind, the sea are here both useful and attractive. Notable in Pliny's description of his baths is the notion that the best of two worlds, nature and art, is available to him:

> ... frigidaria... abunde capacia, si mare in proximo cogites (11).[83]

Here one can combine the pleasures of bathing in artificial pools and in the sea, and, what is more, the bathers can all the while enjoy an attractive vista:

> ... cohaeret calida piscina mirifica, ex qua natantes mare aspiciunt... (11)

Perhaps this possibility of viewing the sea while bathing not in it but in baths constructed by man, is all the more charming because inherent in it is a strong element of illusion. The bather in the *piscina* may choose to think that he is, indeed, in the sea. And as we continue reading this passage, our sense of illusion is strengthened. Pliny tells us how *duo baptisteria velut eiecta sinuantur*: part of the baths must have been built in a daring and surprising way, as if not entirely belonging to the building itself, yet still obviously part of it.

The sense of yielding to illusion becomes quite extraordinary when we read those parts of the Epistle in which Pliny praises the views which open from various vantage points at his estate. Already in dealing with the approach to the villa he remarks (3) that landscape at Laurentum is most varied.[84] The arrangement of windows and doors at his house, we find, makes nature look even more varied than she really is: woods and mountains, the inner portions of the house, as well as the sea, can all be viewed from the same dining room. With the help of three different apertures, the sea is made to look like three different seas:

> Undique valvas aut fenestras non minores valvis habet atque ita a
> lateribus a fronte quasi tria maria prospectat; a tergo cavaedium

---

[83] I assume that the reading *mare* is correct. It is contained in most of the MSS.
[84] Such diversity he also stresses in 5. 6 and elsewhere.

porticum aream porticum rursus, mox atrium silvas et longinquos respicit montes (5).

To the fearful a different room offers sight of the sea from a safer distance (6). For a large panorama of the sea and the coast, one goes up into a kind of tower (12), while from another portion of the building one can look at[85] — not the sea but *hortus... pinguis et rusticus* (15), a vegetable garden. This view may well have been planned as a surprise to an elegant visitor — it does surprise the reader.

Pliny's villa, then, has picture windows arranged so that one can choose to see any one of a great number of totally different aspects of nature: land and sea, gentle nature or fierce; or else one may see the whole variety at once from the tower. Yet the ultimate in easeful enjoyment is depicted in section 21 of the Epistle:

> Lectum et duas cathedras capit [zotheca]; a pedibus mare, a tergo villae, a capite silvae: tot facies locorum totidem fenestris et distinguit et miscet.

Here once more the author is enjoying himself in a very relaxed way, as he did when fishing from his terrace. In the previous passage, however, he created the impression of happiness in the midst of supreme comfort. Here he does more: master of the villa, here he appears to be master over the surrounding nature as well, capable of affecting the landscape to please himself (*et distinguit et miscet*), building what he would like to see out of what is actually available.

In short, villas such as Pliny's own or those of his neighbors exhibit such a mixture of urban and natural features that they appear — another instance of illusion — to be cities (27). This comparison comes at the culmination of Pliny's description and forms his greatest compliment to the villas and their possessors.

Another Epistle, 5. 6, furnishes us with a similarly detailed description of a country estate. Here too we read about exposure to the sun (sections 15, 24, 26, 33) and use of shade (22, 33), about bedrooms impermeable to light and sound (21), as well as about a kind of corridor valued as a reservoir of cool air (30). Again we are told about a variety of attractive views which can be relished without undue effort: one of the best of them can be seen from a hill so easily climbed that the ascent is scarcely felt (14). But while in 2. 17 Pliny paid his attention chiefly to the house, here he devotes the greater part of his essay to the garden and has much to say on the ways in which nature

---

[85] *Ut parva magnis,* as Pliny says elsewhere (5. 6. 44).

is not just viewed but made to penetrate into the house—or appears to penetrate into it.

Pliny greatly enjoys those striking instances of the gardener's art which leave nature looking totally unlike herself. With great pleasure he mentions hedges clipped to form geometrical and even animal figures (16), or else letters and obelisks (35), as well as dwarf shrubs. An inner court contains a bit of the outdoors, some trees and a fountain, within its walls (20),[86] and there are marvellously elaborated fountains on the other parts of the grounds too. They cater to the eye as well as the ear (24). In one and the same suite of rooms there are some chambers which no sound can penetrate (21), and one which holds within itself a small fountain with its *iucundissimum murmur* (23). This *murmur* is not product of nature, we learn: it is achieved by controlling the water properly in a combination of pipes. Finally, there is even a fountain gushing out of a bench, and those who rest there can entertain the illusion that the water is forced out by their weight:

> Ex stibadio aqua velut expressa cubantium pondere sipunculis effluit, cavato lapide suscipitur, gracili marmore continetur atque ita occulte temperatur, ut impleat nec redundet (36).

As if this were not enough of an illusion, Pliny goes on to describe what happens when he uses the bench as a dining couch. Some of the dishes are then put on the edge of the basin (perhaps to make use of the cooling properties of the water), while others, shaped like little boats and birds, are allowed to swim about the surface. With artificial waterfowl and boats on its surface, the basin seems to form a charming illusory substitute for the sea, a varied view of which was so much recommended in the description of the dining rooms of *Epistle* 2. 17.[87]

The fairy-tale atmosphere of the essay increases as we progress into a near-by room where the master of the house is at liberty fully to abandon himself to illusion:

> Marmore splendet, valvis in viridia prominet et exit, alia viridia superioribus inferioribusque fenestris suspicit despicitque. Mox zothecula refugit quasi in cubiculum idem atque aliud. Lectus hic et undique fenestrae, et tamen lumen obscurum umbra premente. Nam laetissima

---

[86] We remember how Statius' patron Manilius Vopiscus built his house around a tree in order to spare it, *Silv.* 1. 3. 59-63.

[87] The ease of controlling such fountains is noted in sect. 40 of *Epist.* 5. 6, where the master of the house appears to lord it over nature by watering his grounds when he pleases.

> vitis per omne tectum in culmen nititur et ascendit. Non secus ibi quam
> in nemore iaceas, imbrem tantum tamquam in nemore non sentias. Hic
> quoque fons nascitur simulque subducitur ... (38-40)

Here is improvement on nature, indeed: the impression of being in the
forest without the attendant inconvenience of getting wet in a shower!
Nature has been made to yield her pleasures without the hardships
often connected with them.

In her pristine, unchanged state, nature is mentioned only for the
sake of the contrast she affords to the contrived and elaborate gardens.
A neighboring meadow elicits the following comment:

> Pratum inde non minus natura quam superiora illa arte visendum (18),

but we may wonder if this meadow is, in fact, genuine, for the essay
mentions how in the midst of clipped hedges, there unexpectedly
appears

> ... in opere urbanissimo subita velut illati ruris imitatio (35).

For all we know, the meadow too may be *imitatio* rather than the real
thing: a lawn, perhaps, instead of a pasture.[88]

Indeed, illusion is kept so prominent at this villa that many of the
available views are altogether fake. Consider the following passage:

> Est et aliud cubiculum a proxima platano viride et umbrosum, marmore
> excultum podio tenus, nec cedit gratiae marmoris ramos insidentesque
> ramis aves imitata pictura.[89] Fonticulus in hoc, in fonte crater ... (22-3)

The chamber is shady and filled with a greenish kind of light, like
some forest glade. Yet the branches overhead, just as are the birds
perching in them, are painted, not real, and instead of a natural rivulet
we have here an artificial fountain. As in the bedchamber (38-40, see
above), so here nature can be enjoyed entirely indoors. And in still
another room we find a view of the outside vineyards taken, as it were,
into the house, so tangible and close are the plantings. It becomes
impossible to tell what is actually inside and what outside:

> A latere aestiva cryptoporticus in edito posita, quae non adspicere vineas
> sed tangere videtur ... post latissimis fenestris vineas, valvis aeque vineas
> sed per cryptoporticum quasi admittit (29).

[88] Precisely what Pliny means by *imitatio* in this instance is difficult to tell, but the
general thought seems clear: he is speaking of a surprising, delightful mixture of the
civilized and the rustic. It is worth comparing the present passage with what he says in
6. 31. 17, where a pier in the process of construction is eventually to be masked so as
to appear like *enata insula*, a natural island.

[89] See Sherwin-White *ad locum*.

To sum up, illusion or imitation of nature can for Pliny be as good, or even better, than nature herself.[90]

In subsequent centuries, while the political vicissitudes of the Empire had not yet destroyed the magnificence of her technical accomplishments, poets continued praising villas, baths, and aqueducts. Frequently we find evidence that these later writers sought to imitate Statius' and Pliny's efforts of the same kind. Outstanding among them were Ausonius and Rutilius, whom we shall discuss before passing on to Sidonius Apollinaris, who is inferior, as well as later, than they.

In *De Herediolo* 29-32, Ausonius reveals his liking for the comforts of a well-appointed household. In *Ordo Urbium Nobilium* his interests expand to embrace urban comforts. Interesting for our purposes are especially lines 135-44, devoted to Bordeaux, a well-planned city with straight streets and, most remarkably (145-62), a spring of water, made to serve man. Ausonius admires the spring not as nature's (or God's) handiwork but as one of the outstanding features of comfortable urban life: the source of the water supply necessary for the convenience of the inhabitants. When, elsewhere in the same poem, he speaks of Milan, he finds it too a very pleasant place, for it too is well inhabited and the people who live there are clever and keep their houses in good repair:

> ... innumerae cultaeque domus, facunda virorum
> ingenia et mores laeti ... (36-7)

As he writes these lines he seems to echo Statius' approval of cultivated, inhabited places, and his feeling that only a lived-in landscape is truly attractive:

> ... innumerae gaudentia rura superne
> insedere domus ... (*Silv.* 3. 1. 78-9)[91]

Like Statius, Ausonius feels a love for civilization and turns his feelings into art.

The poem in which Ausonius best expresses his attitude toward nature and man's place in it is the *Mosella*. The subject matter here

---

[90] Very different from this attitude is Juvenal's criticism of grottoes *dissimiles veris*, *Sat.* 3. 17-20.

[91] Silius Italicus, 14. 646, also uses the expression *innumerae domus* (in the accusative), but with no marked delight in prosperous, civilized communities.

gives him full scope to picture nature as a servant of man. At the beginning of the poem, we read how Ausonius toils travelling to the Moselle valley through pathless, uncultivated regions in which he clearly is ill at ease:

> ... iter ingrediens nemorosa per avia solum
> et nulla humani spectans vestigia cultus
> praetereo arentem sitientibus undique terris
> Dumnissum riguasque perenni fonte Tabernas
> arvaque Sauromatum nuper metata colonis,
> et tandem primis Belgarum conspicor oris
> Noiomagum, divi castra inclita Constantini (5-11).

After emerging from the wilderness, Ausonius characterizes the town of Noviomagus in terms reminiscent of a Virgilian passage dealing with the abodes of the blest (*Aen.* 6. 640-1):

> Purior hic campis aer Phoebusque sereno
> lumine purpureum reserat iam sudus Olympum (12-3).

Here, in a civilized region, the forests have been cleared and, consequently,

> nec iam consertis per mutua vincula ramis
> quaeritur exclusum viridi caligine caelum
> sed liquidum iubar et rutilam visentibus aethram
> libera perspicui non invidet aura diei (14-7).[92]

The woods cut down, nature assumes a much happier guise. Their wild aspect appears to Ausonius to be altogether unenjoyable, hostile to the expanse of the sky itself.

After these introductory lines, the remainder of the poem deals with the sights along the Moselle, which the reader views through the

---

[92] Numerous passages in Latin authors can have provided material for these lines. (See the parallels given by Carl Hosius, *Die Moselgedichte des Decimus Magnus Ausonius und des Venantius Fortunatus*, 3rd ed., Marburg 1926.) None of them, however, contains language as strongly hyperbolic as do the verses of Statius:

> Vix ramis locus, agrestes adeo omnia cingunt
> exuviae, et viridem ferri nitor impedit umbram (*Th.* 9. 591-2);
> ...maeret onyx, longe queriturque exclusus ophites (*Silv.* 1. 5. 35).

Other writers (for instance, Curtius Rufus, 4. 7. 16) wrote of sunlight scarcely able to penetrate a deep shade, but did not say that there was scarcely room for branches in the dense crown of the forest. This piece of exaggeration seems rather unusual and may well have influenced Ausonius. (There is no need for Barth's emendation *radiis* for *ramis* in *Th.* 9. 591.) Equally hyperbolic is the second Statian parallel, taken from the poet's description of the incomparably splendid baths of Claudius Etruscus, for which the builders have used only the most expensive and luxurious materials. Ausonius transfers to the sky over the Moselle the affective words in which Statius mentioned the cast-off materials. The sky is so enamoured of the earth that it mourns its inability to cope with the dense branches of the uncultivated forest which conceal the earth from it.

author's eyes, that is, either from a boat (as in 150-1) or from some point on the banks. The comfortable villas along the river are introduced into the poem mainly as vantage points (283-4) from which one can view the life along and on the Moselle: the fishing, the rowing contests, and all the rest. It would seem not that the poet is travelling but that he is letting life pass by him. He—and the reader—do not participate in the described activity. They are passive spectators at a performance. Indeed, in speaking of the vineyards, Ausonius compares their plantations to a natural theater (156). He is not really concerned with nature as she is, but as she can, and does, appear to the civilized inhabitant of this civilized part of Gaul.

Therefore, throughout the poem much is made of the illusions which delight Ausonius' eye and ear as he contemplates the river. Remarkable descriptions of audial illusion occur in lines 168-9 and 296-7, while of optical illusion there are almost innumerable instances. Particularly fond Ausonius seems of sense impressions produced by the deceptive nature of water. He lovingly tells of the way pebbles seen through water look like precious stones (65-74), about the reflections of the surrounding scenery in the Moselle (186-99), about people intrigued by their own reflections (225-9, 230-9).[93] The realm of illusion extends into much of the activity that the poet witnesses—activity which, on the surface of it, may appear real enough: a contest he sees is but a mock combat (200-39); schools of fish, *ignara doli, decepta examina*, are deluded by a fisherman (240-56), who is presently himself deluded into the belief that he can catch the escaped fish by diving after them (270-5), like Glaucus, that ambiguous mythological creature, not quite man, not quite fish (276-82). The poet is dwelling in an unreal world whose activity is closer to play than to the seriousness of real life, and like the shepherd of the Virgilian pastoral (*Ecl.* 7. 17), he

> ... sua seria ludo
> posthabet: excludit veteres nova gratia curas (206-7).

Even though he has dismissed luxury and declared a preference for *naturae opus* (48-52), what Ausonius means by such love of nature has

---

[93] Frequently the poet stresses in these passages the tenuousness of the distinction between what is and what is not real:

> Ipsa suo gaudet simulamine nautica pubes,
> fallaces fluvio mirata redire figuras (228-9);
> ... laeta ignorato fruitur virguncula ludo (233);
> ... ad umbrarum ludibria nautica pubes
> ambiguis fruitur veri falsique figuris (238-9).

nothing to do with his uncomfortable trek through the woods. Aside from his pleasure in echoes and reflections,[94] what he likes most about the Moselle is her civilized aspect: the vineyards, the river traffic, the mills and stonecutters' yards (361-4), the villas and baths. When he reports in entrancing detail what fish are native to the Moselle, he does enjoy their appearance and movements, but their palatability is his main concern. Even passages emphasizing the beauty of the fish contain distracting particulars which remind the reader of the culinary side of the subject; for instance, in mentioning the *mustela*, Ausonius says:

> Quis te naturae pinxit color! Atra superne
> puncta notant tergum, qua lutea circuit iris,
> lubrica caeruleus perducit tergora fucus.
> Corporis ad medium pinguescis, at illinc
> usque sub extremam squalet cutis arida caudam (110-4).

The lovely colors of the fish are relatively unimportant. What matters most is to determine how fat the fish are, and in which parts of their bodies.

Picturing the villas along the banks of the river, Ausonius unrestrainedly takes from Statius, when not the actual wording of his poems,[95] then at least a whole host of themes: the villas themselves, their baths, the mild climate of this region, the Satyrs frolicking around human dwellings. Like Statius, Ausonius does not look to nature for indications of a Golden Age, either past or future, or for primitive simplicity. Instead, he prefers nature urbanized and cultured, landscapes filled with domiciles and baths, artifice which creates effects almost natural yet hardly to be expected in the natural state. Life amid rusticity is at its best when nature is placid and helpful, and the natural convenience of the terrain augmented with the help of

---

[94] One can argue that such a pleasure is quite removed from true love of nature, since it seeks not natural objects as they really are but as they imitate other things.

[95] There is, indeed, plentiful direct borrowing of words and phrases, as well as borrowing of themes. In his dependence on Statius' language, Ausonius takes material not only from the *Silvae* but also from the descriptions contained in Statius' epics. For instance, we seem to hear Statius' salutation to Lemnos in Ausonius' address to the Moselle:

> Salve, amnis laudate agris, laudate colonis,
> dignata imperio debent cui moenia Belgae (*Mos.* 23-4).

> Insula dives agris opibusque armisque virisque,
> nota situ et Getico nuper ditata triumpho (*Th.* 5. 305-6).

Both these places are attractive because they are civilized: rich in fields and the tillers of fields, and witnesses to Rome's triumphs over the barbarian.

architecture. We remember how Statius spoke of a villa built on the two sides of a stream:

> Litus utrumque domi, nec te mitissimus amnis
> dividit. Alternas servant praetoria ripas,
> non externa sibi fluviorum obstare queruntur
> Sestiacos nunc Fama sinus pelagusque natatum
> iactet et audaci victos delphinas ephebo!
> Hic aeterna quies, nullis hic iura procellis,
> numquam fervor aquis. Datur hic transmittere visus
> et voces et paene manus...
> Quid referam alternas gemino super aggere mensas...
>
> (*Silv.* 1. 3. 24-9, 64)

While Ausonius is by no means slavishly dependent on Statius' vocabulary, he inserts a similar description into his poem, and expresses a contempt like to Statius' for the same mythological *topos* which Statius mentioned: the straits separating Sestos from Abydos, and the effort and tragedy to which these straits were witness:

> ... [villas] medius dirimit sinuosis flexibus errans
> amnis, et alternas comunt praetoria ripas.
> Quis modo Sestiacum pelagus, Nepheleidos Helles
> aequor, Abydeni freta quis miretur ephebi?
> Quis Chalcedonio constratum ab litore pontum,
> regis opus magni, mediis euripus ubi undis
> Europaeque Asiaeque vetat concurrere terras?
> Non hic dira freti rabies, non saeva furentum
> proelia caurorum; licet hic commercia linguae
> iungere et alterno sermonem texere pulsu.
> Blanda salutiferas permiscunt litora voces,
> et voces et paene manus: resonantia utrimque
> verba refert mediis concurrens fluctibus echo (*Mos.* 285-97).[96]

---

[96] The similarity of attitude in the two passages has been noted before. Cf. Hosius' commentary on that of Ausonius:

> Hier... bemerken wir eine äusserst starke Benutzung der Statianischen Beschreibung der Villa Tiburtina... der vielleicht die Verse 287-97 eine nachträgliche Einfügung verdanken. Denn V. 298 schliesst sich viel ungezwungener an 286, als an seine unmittelbaren Vorgänger an.

It is quite possible that Hosius is right, and that Ausonius inserted these lines into his poem after he had once more (or perhaps for the first time?) come into contact with *Silv.* 1. 3. Yet, as Hosius recognizes, they testify to their author's thorough acquaintance with other of Statius' works as well. From *Silv.* 1. 3, as we have seen, he has taken the friendly stream, the *praetoria,* the strait of Abydos and its connection with Leander, the quiet, the ease with which the people on the opposite banks can converse, the near possibility of reaching hands across the stream. But while Ausonius is speaking about the Hellespont, a passage from Statius' *Achilleid* occurs to him, because it too refers to

For both poets the country houses of the rich are a background to a quiet, civilized friendship—a background to happiness. Externally too the villas they describe are similar. Those on the Moselle are supported by numberless columns, *innumeris... super nitentia tecta columnis* (336), as were the palaces of Statius' description (*Silv.* 1. 2. 152, *innumeris fastigia nixa columnis*).[97] One of the villas stands *natura sublimis* (*Mos.* 321) on a rock, another is placed *fundata crepidine ripae* (*Mos.* 322),[98] yet another *refugit captumque sinu sibi vindicat amnem* (323). Still other houses make up for their low position by being built high up into a semblance of a mountain (327-30).

Human comfort and delectation are here of paramount importance. The inhabitants of these artificial mountains enjoy fish kept in surroundings resembling the natural (331-2), and have their *atria* in charming proximity to the real outdoors (*atria quid memorem viridantibus adsita pratis*, 335). The villas are placed high so as to offer a good view to their inhabitants; the fish are well accommodated so that they may lose none of their natural savor by the time when they are eaten. Man continues to manipulate nature as he will, and as he did in Statius' time.

Ausonius' emphasis on comfort culminates (as it seems also to do in the *Silvae*) in his description of Roman baths. These abound along the river, and Ausonius describes them in fond detail borrowed from Statius' reports of similar baths in Italy. To show how close the resemblance is, it is sufficient simply to indicate the various particulars in which Ausonius, frequently displaying strong verbal parallelism to Statius, imitates his source. The baths are situated on a slope of the river bank (*Mos.* 332, *Silv.* 1. 3. 43); the poet describes how they exude smoke (*Mos.* 337, *Silv.* 2. 3. 17) and how steam rolls down from them (*Mos.* 339-40, *Silv.* 1. 5. 59). Even someone who has seen Baiae would be impressed with such baths as these (*Mos.* 345-8, *Silv.* 1. 5. 60-1), and both poets insist how convenient it is to mix the delights of bathing

---

the Hellespont. He takes from it a whole phrase, *Europam Asiamque vetat*, making only a slight alteration in case (cf. also Ausonius *Epist.* 23. 17-21):

   ...Phrixi qua semita iungi
   Europamque Asiamque vetat... (*Ach.* 1. 409-10)

   Europaeque Asiaeque vetat concurrere terras (*Mos.* 291).

We ought also to note that the two descriptions of villas end similarly: *quid referam*, says Statius (64); Ausonius echoes him: *quid memorem* (335).

[97] Cf. Martial (2. 14. 9), *centum pendentia tecta columnis,* and other similar passages given by Hosius *ad locum.*

[98] Cf. Statius *Silv.* 1. 3. 43.

in these edifices and in the more natural way, in the river (*Mos.* 341-4, *vivis aquis, Silv.* 1. 5. 51-4, *amnis vivit*), where, as Ausonius' choice of words indicates, one goes for the sake of variety as well as comfort:

> Vidi ego defessos multo sudore lavacri
> fastidisse lacus et frigora piscinarum,
> ut vivis fruerentur aquis, mox amne refotos
> plaudenti gelidum flumen pepulisse natatu.[99]

At the end of the poem (381-414), Ausonius declares that men are the best product of the beneficent country around the Moselle — men upright and brave and excellent in every way.[100] Throughout the poem, the emphasis has been on man and what is good and pleasurable for man, and thus the praise of man forms an appropriate conclusion to the *Mosella.*

It is hardly surprising that Rutilius Namatianus, who in *De Reditu Suo* frequently regrets the past glories of pagan Rome, just as frequently celebrates Rome's engineering and architectural accomplishments, many of them, alas, falling into ruin. Some two generations after Ausonius' journey on the Moselle, Italy, unlike Ausonius' flourishing Gaul, is in a sorry state, and Rutilius' reason for returning to Gaul by sea is that the roads across dry land are so bad:

> Electum pelagus, quoniam terrena viarum
> plana madent fluviis, cautibus alta rigent.
> Postquam Tuscus ager postquamque Aurelius agger,
> perpessus Geticas ense vel igne manus,
> non silvas domibus, non flumina ponte coercet,
> incerto satius credere vela mari (37-42).

But before he leaves, he addresses to the City a speech full of passionate love and admiration, a speech in which the praise of Rome's tectonic marvels is by no means the least important topic. An enumeration of the buildings of Rome is a task involving great effort, but Rutilius approaches it with the help of Statius as his occasional model:

> Percensere labor densis decora alta trophaeis,
> ut si quis stellas pernumerare velit (1. 93-4).

---

[99] Of course, taken literally, the word *plaudenti* refers to the resounding stroke of the swimmers, but it may, within this cheerful context, assume also a secondary meaning, that of approbation. — Cf. *Silv.* 1. 3. 70-4, where the Anio *plaudit aquas* as he takes a swim at night.

[100] This sentiment reminds the reader of Virgil *G.* 2. 173ff, a passage in which Virgil's praise of Italy culminates.

We remember that Statius experienced similar difficulties in enumerating and praising the rich decorations of a friend's house, and that he too approached his task with the phrase *labor est*:

> ...Labor est auri memorare figuras
> aut ebur aut dignas digitis contingere gemmas (*Silv.* 1. 3. 48-9).

Indeed, Statius' task had much in common with that of Rutilius, and it is appropriate that Rutilius' admiration for Roman buildings should lead him to admire and thus imitate the poet who, before him, most eloquently dealt with the same themes. The remoteness of Rutilius' model by some three centuries serves perhaps all the better to illustrate for the reader, and to convince the author himself, of the perpetuity of the magnificent works he extols. For magnificent Rome is, and even the sky over her is different and better than elsewhere, or as Rutilius himself hyperbolically, yet somehow convincingly, says later on,

> ...Caeli plaga candidior tractusque serenus
> signat septenis culmina clara iugis.
> Illic perpetui soles atque ipse videtur
> quem sibi Roma facit purior esse dies (1. 197-200).[101]

Let us quote at some length what he has to say about Rome as the marvel of the world:

> Quid loquar aerio pendentes fornice rivos,
> qua vix imbriferas tolleret Iris aquas?
> Hos potius dicas crevisse in sidera montes;
> tale giganteum Graecia laudet opus.
> Intercepta tuis conduntur flumina muris;
> consumunt totos celsa lavacra lacus.
> Nec minus et propriis celebrantur roscida venis
> totaque nativo moenia fonte sonant.
> Frigidus aestivas hinc temperat halitus auras,
> innocuamque levat purior unda sitim...
> Quid loquar inclusas inter laquearia silvas,
> vernula qua vario carmine ludit avis?
> Vere tuo numquam mulceri desinit annus;
> deliciasque tuas victa tuetur hiemps (1. 97-106, 111-4).

Here we have a picture of nature completely coerced into man's service, and that on a grandiose scale. "Streams suspended in air" is Rutilius' name for aqueducts. These streams are almost entirely manmade, and better than what Nature has provided, for by their

---

[101] The expression *septem culmina* for Rome seems to come from Statius, *Silv.* 1. 5. 23 or 1. 1. 64.

means irrigation reaches areas inaccessible to Iris. And yet the name of streams seems insufficient for the great aqueducts, and Rutilius presently changes his nomenclature and calls them mountains, bringing before the reader's mind still other huge works of nature, or, as mythology has it, of the Giants. The aqueducts are artificial mountains and artificial streams at the same time, and at least the equals of such powers of nature as the rain, with its harbinger the rainbow. The aqueduct and the rainbow are set here side by side, just as the rainbow and an arch find themselves compared at the beginning of Statius' poem dealing with the Via Domitia:

> Huius ianua prosperumque limen
> arcus, belligeris ducis tropaeis
> et totis Ligurum nitens metallis,
> quantus nubila qui coronat imbri (*Silv.* 4. 3. 97-100).[102]

Yet technology is for Rutilius not so superior to nature that nature should be totally disregarded. As have his predecessors, so he too praises the attractive combination of nature and art. Human skill has introduced into Rome huge bodies of water, but the City is blessed with her own natural springs as well:

> Nec minus et propriis celebrantur roscida venis
> totaque nativo moenia fonte sonant.

Still, these springs, the work of nature unmixed with art, find praise chiefly for utilitarian reasons: as we learn from the next few lines, they alleviate heat and thirst.

Lines 111-4 speak of an especially amazing mixture of nature and civilization. Whole woods, birds and all, are enclosed within the courtyards of palaces for the delectation of their owners, who thus not only have nature within their very houses but even command the

---

[102] As he goes on to point out how whole rivers and, indeed, lakes, have been brought by man's skill within the City's confines, Rutilius, his imagination still busy with the picture of the toiling Giants, borrows a word from a passage of Statius' *Thebaid,* which also deals with giants (the Cyclopes, to be precise) as builders:

> ...camposque et celsa Cyclopum
> tecta superiecto nebularum incendit amictu [Apollo] (*Th.* 1. 630-1).

The context of the two passages is somewhat dissimilar. Both poets speak of very impressive structures, but Rutilius is dealing with baths, Statius with the buildings of the Cyclopes; Rutilius is full of admiration for the structures he describes, but Statius points to the remarkable feat of Apollo, in comparison with which the roofs of the Cyclopes become insignificant. The phrase *celsa lavacra* is the subject of Rutilius' sentence, while *celsa tecta* is a direct object in the passage from the *Thebaid.* Yet by echoing Statius' mythological description, Rutilius seems to have in mind some parallel between the goddess Rome and Apollo: both of them surpass the works of the Giants.

change of the seasons in these groves, as in greenhouses, and keep up in them a perpetual spring.[103]

As Rutilius casts a final glance at Rome, which is already becoming faint in the distance, he describes this last view of the City in terms reminiscent of two passages of the *Silvae*, both also dealing with objects at great distance from the viewer:[104]

> Respectare iuvat vicinam saepius urbem
> et montes visu deficiente sequi (1. 189-90);

> ... vix lumine fesso
> explores quam longus in hunc despectus ab alto (*Silv.* 1. 1. 87-8);

> longa super species: fessis vix culmina prendas
> visibus auratique putes laquearia caeli (*Silv.* 4. 2. 30-1).

The Statian echoes in this instance become particularly meaningful if we bear in mind that Rutilius is now painfully taking leave of Rome with all her marvels, while the passages he seems to recollect from the *Silvae* deal precisely with these marvels: the one with the equestrian statue of Domitian, the other with Domitian's palace.

A distant din still seems to reach Rutilius. It is the noise of yet another feature of urban civilization, the circus, and it forms his last contact with the city life he so loves:

> Saepius attonitae resonant Circensibus aures;
> nuntiat accensus plena theatra favor.
> Pulsato notae redduntur ab aethere voces,
> vel quia perveniunt vel quia fingit amor (201-4).[105]

---

[103] I take lines 113-4 to be closely connected in meaning with the two previous lines. Later on, in lines 197-200, Rutilius speaks of the happy natural climate of Rome. Here he is dealing with the miracles of her construction, and immediately after line 114, of another human accomplishment: Rome as a military power. Therefore I interpret lines 113-4 as a reference to human control over climate.

[104] Seneca, *Epist.* 89. 2, deals in similar terms with the insufficiency of vision: *visus ... deficit,* but he is pointing out how difficult it is to perceive philosophical truths. He is not speaking of vision in literal terms. Cf. also Rutilius 1. 433-4.

[105] Rutilius' mind is full of Rome, but also full of Statius, even at this point. He seems to be repeating certain words of the *Thebaid* (1. 590-1, 4. 668-9, or 7. 227-8). Although the Statian contexts are different, the imitation reveals Rutilius' close knowledge of the *Thebaid*. Such use of Statian phrases in a totally different context is frequent in *De Reditu*. Thus, for instance, from one of Statius' rustic poems comes the thought that man is very happy in the habitat which is most familiar to him and of which he feels himself to be part:

> Iam iam laxatis carae complexibus urbis
> vincimur, et serum vix toleramus iter (1. 35-6);

> ...in carae vivit complexibus umbrae.
> Hic igitur tibi laeta quies ... (*Silv.* 4. 6. 95-6)

As Rutilius travels on, he discovers that, while the condition of landroads is poor, many harbors are still in good order. He singles out the one at Centumcellae, which, as he possibly may have known, Pliny described while it was being built (6. 31. 15-7). Here is Rutilius' picture of it:

> Ad Centumcellas forti defleximus Austro;
> tranquilla puppes in statione sedent.
> Molibus aequoreum concluditur amphitheatrum,
> angustosque aditus insula facta tegit,
> attollit geminas turres bifodoque meatu
> faucibus artatis pandit utrumque latus.
> Nec posuisse satis laxo navalia portu;
> ne vaga vel tutas ventilet aura rates,
> interior medias sinus invitatus in aedes
> instabilem fixis aera nescit aquis... (237-46)

Pliny too[106] spoke of the intended natural appearance of the artificial island. Rutilius' passage culminates in the description of the way in which human skill has made a placid gulf part of the buildings on the shore, *medias invitatus in aedes* (245). Love of nature and admiration for technology are here combined, as they were in some Statian passages which too spoke of natural bodies of water admitted into human dwellings and made part of them:

> Haec pelagi clamore fremunt, haec tecta sonoros
> ignorant fluctus terraeque silentia malunt (*Silv.* 2. 2. 51-2).

> Hic aeterna quies, nullis hic iura procellis,
> numquam fervor aquis... (*Silv.* 1. 3. 29-30).

A similar wonder and excitement at the union of nature and art finds expression consistently through the two *Silvae* which Rutilius may have recollected as he wrote the lines quoted here.

When he speaks about another resting place on his journey, he again, like Statius, says that he is at a loss whether to praise nature more or art:

> Haec proprios nuper tutata est insula saltus
> sive loci ingenio seu domini genio (1. 327-8).

As we observe, Statius is speaking about a man who enjoys life in the country, where he experiences a happy sense of relaxation. Rutilius portrays himself as a city dweller, so fond of and accustomed to Rome that a trip out of the city's confines tires him and makes him unhappy. He may be twisting Statius' meaning purposely, to show the superiority of Rome to any other place of abode, even a peaceful country retreat.

[106] *Epist.* 6. 31. 16-7; see above. See also footnote 110 on Pliny's influence.

Ingenium quam mite solo! Quae forma beatis
ante manus artemque locis!... (*Silv.* 1. 3. 15-6)

...Quae rerum turba! Locine
ingenium an domini mirer prius? (*Silv.* 2. 2. 44-5)

Among the greatest attractions of a villa which he visits later he lists
a *vivarium*, that most artificial imitation of a natural habitat (377-80).
Still farther along his way, he contemplates the ruins of a fortification
which used to serve as a lighthouse, and on this occasion he speaks in
Statian terms of Pharos, one of the great engineering achievements of
man:

...extollit in aethera moles
lumine nocturno conspicienda Pharos (1. 403-4);

lumina noctivagae tollit Pharus aemula lunae (*Silv.* 3. 5. 101).[107]

*Mira loci facies* (533) says he at yet another harbor (echoing Statius'
wording in *Silv.* 2. 2. 26), which lies close to a villa particularly
admirable because it has been built on an artificially constructed
peninsula (527-31).

Soon after visiting these spots, Rutilius' boat makes an enforced stop
because of bad weather. Rutilius pictures his stay on shore much as
Statius had described a vacation that he took walking in—not the
country, but, again, Rome!

Otia vicinis terimus navalia silvis (1. 621),

says Rutilius, drawing on

...cum patulis tererem vagus otia saeptis
iam moriente die... (*Silv.* 4. 6. 2-3)[108]

This is probably the last Statian *locus* in the poem, which, to the
reader's regret, soon breaks off. As reluctantly as Rutilius lost the sight
of Rome, we lose sight of this inveterate lover of the City and the
urban comforts.

Sidonius Apollinaris expressly points to Statius and Pliny as his
models: Statius' *Silvae*, he says, provide a pattern for his *Carmen* 22
(see 22. 6),[109] while Pliny as well as Pliny's imitator Symmachus are his

---

[107] Statius is here speaking of Pharos generically, calling a lighthouse in the vicinity
of Naples by this name. Rutilius too may be using the name generically, meaning that
no lighthouse existed at Populonia when he passed through it, although the fortifications
that still stood there had previously, indeed, served well as a lighthouse.

[108] Cf. also *Silv.* 3. 5. 61.

[109] *Carmen* 9. 226-9 also evinces Sidonius' fondness for Statius, and the *Silvae* in
particular.

teachers in epistolary composition (see *Epist.* 1. 1. 1).[110] It is true that both Statius' and Pliny's descriptions of country houses give him some material for similar efforts of his own, but Pliny's influence predominates, possibly because Sidonius' view of life is that of a prosaist, even when he writes verse. The technique of Sidonius' composition is somewhat different from that of the authors we have examined above: relatively few words and phrases are directly taken from Pliny and Statius, and his use of such gleanings is, more often than not, infelicitous. Still, the atmosphere of contentment and the love of comfort that pervade his descriptions are not greatly different from what we found in the work of his predecessors.

*Carmen* 22, which deals with a *burgus* belonging to the poet's friend Pontius Leontius, contains numerous echoes of Statius,[111] but the greater part of these stem from Statius' epics, rather than the *Silvae*, the acknowledged source of the poem.[112] Sidonius' description

---

[110] It is strange that Symmachus nowhere imitates Pliny's descriptions of his country houses. In *Epist.* 1. 3 and elsewhere (1. 5, 2. 59, 6. 32, *etc.*; the numbering of his epistles is that employed in Otto Seeck's edition, *MGH* VI 1, Berlin 1883) he speaks of escaping to Baiae or into the country, far away from the crowd, and in 3. 55 and 82 he mentions the pleasure of watching the Tiber traffic from his villa, while 6. 48 contains a brief reference to the advantages of a friend's baths. Aside from these allusions, Symmachus has nothing to say on a subject which was so fully exploited by Pliny, his most important model, as well as by other of his predecessors, such as Ausonius. (In 1. 14 Symmachus speaks with admiration of the *Mosella*, but most of his references to it are limited to the fish enumerated in Ausonius' poem.)

Nor do other epistolographers after Pliny, either pagan or Christian, furnish us with comparably full descriptions of villas. There is nothing of the kind in Fronto, Salvian, Ruricius, Faustus, Avitus, or Ennodius. Sidonius stands alone. This is all the more strange in view of the persuasive articles of Alan Cameron, "The Fate of Pliny's Letters in the Late Empire," *CQ* XV (1965), 289-98, and "Pliny's Letters in the Later Empire. An Addendum," *CQ* XVII (1967), 421-2. Cameron argues against E. T. Merrill, "The Tradition of Pliny's Letters," *CP* X (1915), 8-25, Merrill's preface to his edition of Pliny's letters (Teubner 1922), iii-v, and S. E. Stout, "The Coalescence of the Two Plinys," *TAPA* LXXXVI (1955), 250-5, and demonstrates that Pliny's epistles were popular in late antiquity.

[111] See the index of *loci similes* in Christian Luetjohann's edition, *MGH* VIII (Berlin 1887).

[112] It is difficult to tell what determines Sidonius' choice to imitate particular passages. Perhaps his relative lack of familiarity with pagan authors accounts for his heavy but indiscriminate reliance on the few whom he has read and remembered. Thus, although mythology is not the distinguishing feature of the *Silvae*, he is indebted to these for several of his mythological allusions. For instance, his references to drunkenness, lines 38 and 220, seem to go back to Statius' involved mythological *locus* in *Silv.* 3. 1. 41. Sidonius' knowledge of the cannibal Antiphates, line 2, seems to go no farther back than *Silv.* 1. 3. 84-5 and his invocation of Erato, lines 12 and 20, is taken from Statius' *Silv.* 1. 2. 46-9, the amatory content of which fully justifies the choice of Erato as the presiding Muse. Sidonius' address to her, on the other hand, is completely out of context.

of the variegated marble which embellishes the house of Pontius (137-41) is, indeed, based on the *Silvae*,[113] but while Statius skilfully used such passages to create the picture of a luxurious life which had at its command the best of the natural world, and the world of art as well, no such meaning is apparent in Sidonius, who merely attaches the Statian *panni* because they have struck him as attractive for their own sake, rather than as part of a complex, sophisticated view of man's place in nature. Sidonius' account of Pontius' baths (180-1, 184-6) is very brief and, surprisingly, seems to owe nothing to Statius, although a few lines down (189-91), when he is discussing the heating of Pontius' house, he may have in mind the baths of *Silv.* 1. 5. 58-9.[114]

What Sidonius says about the location of the rooms in the *burgus* is quite close to Pliny's treatment of a similar topic:

> ... [burgus] diem natum cernit sinuamine dextro,
> fronte videns medium, laevo visura cadentem,
> non perdit quicquam trino de cardine caeli
> et totum solem lunata per atria servat (154-7).

This passage resembles Pliny (2. 17. 8, 20, and especially 23), even so far as to echo the words *solem servat*. The word *cadentem* in line 155, a good ending for a hexameter, may come from Statius (*Silv.* 2. 2. 46), but, farther along, line 179 speaks of *aestiva porticus*, as does Pliny (5. 5. 29).

Other topics which he has in common with Pliny, Sidonius treats in considerably different terms. For instance, when he pictures a pond, he says:

> Flecteris ad laevam: te porticus accipit ampla
> directis curvata viis, ubi margine summo
> pendet et artatis stat saxea silva columnis.
> Alta volubilibus patet hic cenatio valvis;

(Yet consider the vexed question regarding the suitability of Virgil's invocation of Erato in *A*. 7. 34-41.)

[113] See passages such as *Silv.* 1. 5. 36-41 and 2. 2. 86-93. Passages on marble in Sidonius' other poems, for instance, *Carm.* 5. 37ff. and 11. 18ff., also owe something to Statius.

[114] Since it is hardly to be supposed that in the Fifth century the one provincial house of Pontius really contained all the different kinds of marble which Statius' patrons owned at their several suburban villas in the age of Domitian, we may assume that not truthfulness but some other consideration prevented Sidonius from imitating not Statius' lists of marble only but his descriptions of baths as well. Perhaps Sidonius exaggerates just where reality falls short of luxury: any well-to-do Roman house, even in the provinces, usually had a bath, but rare varieties of marble would be difficult to procure so far from their places of origin.

fusilis euripus propter; cadit unda superne
ante fores pendente lacu, venamque secuti
undosa inveniunt nantes cenacula pisces (204-10).

Pliny (5. 6. 23) had a similar pond, and it too harbored fish and
boasted a small waterfall, and could be viewed from the windows of
the house. Pliny's wording was completely different and, no doubt,
difficult for Sidonius to take over into his hexameters, but the Fifth
century Christian bishop is still close to the spirit of the passages
written by a pagan senator several hundred years previously. At the
end of his verses on Pontius' pond, he indulges himself in a jest: a
rivulet flows from the pond into the house and provides the
domesticated fish with a passage into the dining room, where they are
meant to end up anyway. An existence reminding us of the Land of
Cockaigne is still possible, and still delightful and amusing, in Gaul
at this troubled period of Roman history, as it was in Italy in
Pliny's day.

The procession of fish into the dining room is not the only instance
in which the mood of make-believe prevails in the life of a country
gentleman like Pontius:

Ne posteritas dubitet, quis conditor extet,
fixus in introitu lapis est; hic nomina signat
auctorum; sed propter aqua, et vestigia pressa
quae rapit et fuso detergit gurgite caenum (142-5).

The names of the founders of the villa are incised in stone near the
entrance. Close-by water conveniently washes away mud and the
tracks of passers-by, and thus does not allow the letters of the
inscription to become unclear through the accumulation of mud or
dust. What is even more convenient, the water also cleans up after
those who have paused to look at the inscription.[115]

Another playful allusion to the extraordinary comforts of the estate
appears in the lines which describe a peculiarly clever arrangement of

---

[115] The meaning of these lines is difficult, but some connection between the two
halves of the statement seems to be established by the conjunction *sed*. An alternate, less
likely, interpretation may be that water will eventually rub out the inscription, and then
wash away even the sand into which the stone with its lettering will have crumbled. But
elsewhere in the poem Sidonius makes no effort to convince his reader of the
impermanence of worldly things, and such a meaning here would hardly be to the taste
of Pontius, who must have been proud of his well-appointed *burgus*. Line 142 implies
no criticism of the founder's wish to be remembered. On the contrary, it confirms the
impression of stability and permanence which the reader is meant to derive from the
prophecy of Apollo, of which these lines form a part.

the local watercourse, by means of which boats are swept from the river into the water reservoirs on the property, and then right into the baths:

> ... fractis saliens e cautibus altum
> excutitur torrens ipsisque aspergine tectis
> impluit ac tollit nautas et saepe iocoso
> ludit naufragio; nam tempestate peracta
> destituit refluens missas in balnea classes (131-5).

The word *iocoso* indicates that the whole performance is a joke meant to be enjoyed by all concerned, and especially by the spectators.[116] We recollect Ausonius' lines on the mock combats on the Moselle, which he watched from one of the villas situated on the surrounding hills (*Mos.* 200-29). Sidonius' emphasis is once more, as it was with Ausonius and with Pliny, on the playful, the indolent, the unexpected, and the illusory aspects of life.

Although those portions of *Carmen* 22 which we have examined are descriptive, the content of this poem is predominantly mythological. Sidonius' more important attempt to picture a country house is contained in a prose essay, *Epist.* 2. 2. Here his faithfulness to Pliny is quite remarkable. Once more he commandeers Statius' list of various kinds of marble,[117] but the rest of the Epistle is all Pliny, or rather an attempt to boast that the author's estate possesses practically all the features that Pliny mentioned when he wrote about his country houses.[118]

The *mons terrenus* near which Sidonius' villa is situated reminds us of Pliny's (5. 6. 8) *terreni colles.* Such proximity to hills offers convenience of a special kind: Pliny told us that, due to the nature of the terrain, *caeduae silvae cum ipso monte descendunt* (5. 6. 8). Sidonius says practically the same thing, and employs similar exaggeration:

> ... si caedua per iugum silva truncetur, in ora fornacis lapsu velut spontaneo deciduis struibus impingitur (4).

Both his and Pliny's possessions boast an *unctorium* (Pliny 2. 17. 11), which Sidonius calls *unguentariae* (4), good plumbing (Pl. 2. 17. 9, Sid. 4), *frigidaria* (2. 17. 11, Sid. 5), a *baptisterium* (2. 17. 11 and 5. 6. 25,

---

[116] See W. B. Anderson's note on this rather vexed passage in his edition of *Sidonius, Poems and Letters* (Harvard, Loeb 1936).

[117] Cf. especially sect. 7 of his letter and *Silv.* 1. 2. 148-51.

[118] Although Sherwin-White, 187, finds that Sidonius' account "is far less complete than that of Pliny. He seems to enlarge only where Pliny was brief."

Sid. 8), a *dormitorium cubiculum* (5. 6. 21, Sid. 10), cool places such as
a *cryptoporticus* (2. 17. 16 and 5. 6. 30, Sid. 10), where the limbs of the
owner find rest (2. 17. 9, Sid. 10), a *diaeta* (5. 17. 15 and 7. 5. 1, Sid.
11), a *cenatio* with a view of a large body of water—the sea in Pliny's
case, a lake in Sidonius' (2. 17. 10 and 12, Sid. 11), a vantage point
from which one can view fishermen (9. 7. 4, Sid. 12),[119] and both have
a waterfall white with foam or spray (5. 6. 24, Sid. 17). Sidonius, as
Pliny before him, attempts to show all of his estate within the space
of a letter, and follows his predecessor also in apologizing for the
lengthy account:

> Vitassem iam dudum ne viderer argutior, nisi proposuissem omnes
> angulos tecum epistula circumire... totam villam oculis tuis subicere
> conamur... non epistula quae describit sed villa quae describitur magna
> est... (Pliny 5. 6. 41, 44)

> ... brevitatem sibi debitam paulo scrupulosior epistula excessit, dum
> totum ruris situm sollicita rimatur; quae tamen summovendi fastidii
> studio nec cuncta perstrinxit. Quapropter bonus arbiter et artifex lector
> non paginam, quae spatia describit, sed villam, quae spatiosa describitur,
> grandem pronuntiabunt (Sid. *Ep.* 2. 2. 20).

Even when Sidonius' villa lacks certain advantages Pliny wrote of,
Sidonius claims to own a substitute. Pliny's dining room and bedrooms
had a view of the sea, Sidonius' rooms look over a lake (2. 17. 6, 10,
12; 5. 6. 28; Sid. 11). Pliny avowed that his *cryptoporticus* was as good
as one built at public expense,

> Hinc cryptoporticus prope publici operis extenditur (2. 17. 16).

Sidonius' cool room is not a real *cryptoporticus*, but it resembles one
well enough:

> A parte vestibuli longitudo tecta intrinsecus patet mediis non interpellata
> parietibus, quae, quia nihil ipsa prospectat, etsi non hippodromus, saltim
> cryptoporticus meo mihi iure vocitabitur (10).

Not only does his remark concerning the coolness of this room recall
a *cryptoporticus* in another of Pliny's letters (5. 6. 30), but so does the
word *hippodromus*. (Pliny speaks of one in 5. 6. 19, 32, 33.) Sidonius'
meaning seems to be: "My possessions are not so grand as to contain
a *hippodromus*, yet I have conveniences of other kinds, such as a
*cryptoporticus* of sorts." In his very confession that this is not a real
*cryptoporticus* but a structure only resembling such, he echoes Pliny,

---

[119] Here we are once more reminded of Ausonius watching life on the Moselle from
the high-lying villas.

whose *cryptoporticus* at the estate mentioned in 5. 6. 30 is but a kind of *subterranea*: "*subest cryptoporticus subterraneae similis.*"[120] And in any case, he confidently says of his *frigidaria* what Pliny did of his *cryptoporticus*:

> ... frigidaria... quae piscinas publicis operibus extructas non impudenter aemularetur (5).

Pliny had a *sphaeristerium* (2. 17. 12, 5. 6. 27). Sidonius does not, properly speaking, possess one, yet he is none the worse off for its absence:

> Ingentes tiliae duae conexis frondibus, fomitibus abiunctis unam umbram non una radice conficiunt. In cuius opacitate, cum me meus Ecdicius inlustrat, pilae vacamus, sed hoc eo usque, donec arborum imago contractior intra spatium ramorum recussa cohibeatur atque illic aleatorium lassis consumpto sphaeristerio faciat (15).

Sidonius enjoys a natural playcourt, made up by the trees on his property: nature makes up for the absence of art. Although his Latin is generally awkward, here it expresses effectively enough a kind of harmony between Sidonius and his natural surroundings.

The illusionistic atmosphere which we have noted in Ausonius' *Mosella*, as well as in some of the earlier writers, finds amusing expression in Sidonius' essay as well. Soon after telling us that firewood marches down the hills straight to his furnaces,[121] Sidonius explains how his baths are lighted. Somehow the light is admitted in such a way that the bathers appear more naked than they would normally:

> Intra conclave succensum solidus dies et haec abundantia lucis inclusae, ut verecundos quosque compellat aliquid se plus putare quam nudos (4).[122]

At the same time, the noise of the water makes the bathers shout in each other's ears to be heard, so that they look funny, as if intent on preserving secrecy in the midst of a crowd:

---

[120] If the correct reading in the above passage from Sidonius is *hypodromus* instead of *hippodromus*, then his meaning is even closer to Pliny's. MSS MCP have *hipodromus*, T has *hypodromus*, F has *ypodromus*.

[121] See above.

[122] Sidonius' account lacks precision but, as we learn from the following section of the letter, the windows in the other bathing areas seem to be located high up, and the walls have a plain white surface. If the *conclave* is similarly appointed, a cold, white light floods the room, making the people in it appear at a disadvantage, the hollows and curves of their bodies more deeply shadowed than they would be in a different kind of light — outdoors, for instance.

Prae strepitu caduci fluminis mutuae vocum vices minus intelleguntur, in aurem sibi populus confabulatur; ita sonitu pressus alieno ridiculum affectat publicus sermo secretum (9).

Even the lions from whose mouths the water falls into the baths reinforce one's sense of being in a world of make-believe. These lions look astonishingly lifelike and give a fright to the unprepared viewer (*temere ingressis*, 8), to the great delight, we suspect, of the master of the house.

In his other works, Sidonius does not have much to say about the beauties or advantages of buildings. *Epist.* 8. 4 lists the good points of a villa, but without going into detail. *Carmen* 24 gives our author occasion to mention how his friend Apollinaris has made his house more comfortable by insulating it from heat by a marble facing (54-5), and how he has indulged himself in building an artificial grotto which the very woods and waters labor to make look natural:

> . . . seu ficto potius specu quiescit
> collis margine, qua nemus reflexum
> nativam dare porticum laborans
> non lucum arboribus facit, sed antrum (65-8).

*Carmina* 18 and 19 are interesting but hyperbolic and very brief reports on Sidonius' baths. In *Epist.* 2. 9. 8 Sidonius has left us an engaging record of the manner in which some of his friends once improvised a crude steambath, but this account is only incidental to the main content of the letter. Finally, in the poem which he inserts into *Epist.* 2. 10, Sidonius, speaking of a Christian church, seems to imply rejection of Roman builders' perpetual search for advantageous exposure to sun. The church is not interested in such things:

> Aedes celsa nitet nec in sinistrum
> aut dextrum trahitur, sed arce frontis
> ortum prospicit aequinoctialem (5-7).

A symbolic orientation, not comfort or pleasure, is the important consideration in building a church. From these lines there is but a step to Christian asceticism and its condemnation of pagan luxuries[123] such

---

[123] This is not to say, of course, that Christian authors had no use for Statius' descriptions, only that they could not very well afford encouraging their readers to indulge in luxurious and indolent habits. Yet when Christian poets such as Prudentius had occasion to describe the luxury of the pagans, they found an excellent model in Statius. Thus, Prudentius pictures a luxurious palace in terms of Statius' description of the royal splendor of Thebes (*Sym.* 2. 838, *Th.* 1. 144), and like many others, he

as cheered the lives of Statius, Pliny, their contemporaries, and their spiritual heirs.

For after Sidonius the themes introduced by Statius well-nigh disappear from literature. Even a worldly poet like Venantius Fortunatus has almost no traces of the long-enduring preoccupations which we have studied in this paper. He writes several poems in praise of various villas, and three dealing with the Moselle (3. 12 and 13, and 10. 9), but those poems addressed to the clergy who own the estates, stress the virtues of the recipients and their zeal in cultivating the land,[124] while the rest are pleasant reading but speak of the lovely landscape or the rich agricultural yield of the farms rather than the achievements of the builder. The longest of the Moselle poems, 10. 9, puts considerable emphasis on the edibles derived directly from the river (67-78), in addition to what the surrounding fields and vineyards furnish. Indeed, in all of Venantius' large literary output there seem to be contained only three poems in which the secular skills of the architect or the engineer merit particular attention.[125] Poem 9. 15 somewhat strangely praises a house built entirely of wood, 3. 10 deals

borrows from Statius' lines on marble (*Sym.* 2. 246-7, *Silv.* 1. 5. 36-40; note also *Silv.* 2. 2. 87-8).

In *Perist.* 10. 266-70 and 291-3, Prudentius reflects Statius' interest in sculpture as an embellishment of a splendid house (*Silv.* 2. 2. 63-8), and the *Apoth.* contains this curious adaptation of a Statian passage dealing with a furnace:

... O proceres, tris vasta incendia anhelis
accepere viros fornacibus, additus unus,
ecce, vaporiferis ridens intersecat ignes.
Filius ille Dei est ... (132-5)

Quaque vaporiferis iunctus fornacibus amnis
ridet anhelantes vicino flumine nymphas? (*Silv.* 1. 3. 45-6)

(See Sister S. M. Hanley, *Classical Sources of Prudentius*, Diss. Cornell 1959, for this and other instances of Prudentius' imitation of Statius.) What used to be part of that epitome of leisurely good life, the pagan baths, has now become an instrument of sin, of torture for the faithful—the Babylonian fiery furnace.

Other Christian poets also occasionally deal with architecture and gardening. Ennodius, for instance, in *Carm.* 2. 19 has as his topic a marble lion whose open mouth discharges the water supply of a house. (*Carm.* 2. 149 is also about a fountain.) *Carm.* 2. 44 and 45, and 2. 111 describe some gardens, but do so in brief and conventional terms. Brief and conventional are also other poets' treatments of such themes. Among the Christian prose authors, Cassiodorus (*Inst.* 1. 29) stands out in commending the amenities that make life easier: baths, fishponds, and the like, but there seems to be no detectable influence of either Statius or Pliny on his description of Vivarium.

[124] For instance, 3. 12 or 1. 18-20.
[125] We are not concerned with the descriptions of the architecture of Christian churches. Of these Venantius has many.

with a man named Felix, who changed the course of a river, and 1. 19 devotes a few lines to an unusually impressive edifice.[126] Of these poems, 3. 10 and 9. 15 are short and not really interested in the technical side of the undertaking described, nor in the delights it provides. 3. 10 is in direct line of descent from those very numerous ancient literary productions which capitalized on the topic of *adynaton*,[127] while 9. 15 may owe something to Statius, directly or indirectly in its use of the formulaic *cedat* to introduce its amplification:[128] let stone now yield to wood. But of Statian spirit it contains nothing.

Only lines 9-14 of poem 1. 19 convey a brief, pallid, but pleasant recollection of the Roman technological achievements, which by this time begin everywhere to fall into disuse:

Machina celsa casae triplici suspenditur arcu,
quo pelagi pictas currere credis aquas.
Exilit unda latens vivo generata metallo,
dulcis et inriguo fonte perennis aquae,
quo super accumbens celebrat convivia pastor
inclusoque lacu pisce natante bibit.[129]

---

[126] Cf. also Venantius *Carm*. 3. 12, a portion of which, 21-42, is concerned with the civilizing influence of man on nature.

[127] Direct antecedents to his poem do not readily come to mind, but the instances of the *topos* here present are a myriad.

[128] Curtius, p. 171, states that Statius established this formula in Latin poetry.

[129] Even though the present investigations do not extend beyound Venantius, it may be appropriate at this point to remind the reader how fashionable and successful the fantastic conceits of the architect and the gardener were in some later ages, and particularly in the heighday of Mannerism. See John Shearman, *Mannerism* (Penguin Books 1967), 123-33. P. 126, in speaking of some extravaganzas of the 16th century, Shearman says:

> The visitor can amuse himself by speculating whether [a grotto] represents a cave cut in architectural form out of the rock, or, alternatively, architecture overlaid with the dense accretions of time. He is not enlightened by groups of naturalistic animals that come to the fountains to drink, or by the birds that perch on the walls. This diverting duality is well expressed in an inscription on a casino at Bomarzo that was built already leaning rather more than the tower at Pisa: "Tell me then whether all these marvels were made to deceive, or are they art?"

The spirit of such fancies goes back to the Roman Empire, and probably owes something directly to it.

Even in the utilitarian first half of the 20th century, accomplishments such as Frank Lloyd Wright's "Falling Water" in Bear Run, Pennsylvania, can serve as instances of a continuing trend to obliterate the dividing line between the natural and the artificial and to please the beholder by creating the illusion that a house is part of nature, even while the comforts of civilization are far from neglected by the builder. And, to descend to the level of popular culture, everywhere in the United States (and probably elsewhere) one can readily observe groups of mass-produced plastic ducks and ducklings, or hens and chickens, displayed on their lawns by suburban lovers of illusion who have, however, never heard of Statius or Pliny.

Printed in the United States
By Bookmasters